Xing Yi Quan Xue
The Study of Form-Mind Boxing

by Sun Lu Tang

Translated by Albert Liu
Compiled and Edited by Dan Miller

Xing Yi Quan Xue
The Study of Form-Mind Boxing

Copyright. © 1993 Albert Liu
ISBN 0-865681-85-6
All Rights Reserved

M E D I A

4635 McEwen Rd. Dallas, Texas 75244
239-280-2380
www.beckettmedia.com

Printed in the United States of America

Disclaimer

The author, translator, and publisher of the book are not responsible for any injury which may result from following the instructions contained herein.

Before embarking on any of the physical activities described in this book, the reader should consult his or her physician for advice regarding their individual suitability for performing such activity.

Table of Contents

The Study of the Five Fists of Xing Yi Quan 81

The Study of Advancing and Retreating: Linking the Five Fists 117

The Study of Wu Xing Pounding of the Creative and Destructive Five Fists 133

Part Two - The Study of the Xing Yi Twelve Forms Derived From Heaven and Earth 147

Editor's Acknowledgments

I would like to acknowledge a number of individuals who made this book possible. First and foremost, I would like to thank Albert Liu for his fine translation of Sun Lu Tang's original text and his wife Jane Yao for helping him with his effort. Jeff Stubbins lent Albert Liu a computer and helped Mr. Liu learn how to use it. Jeff also organized the material that Mr. Liu entered into the computer so that it was properly formatted on the computer disks before it was sent to the publisher.

I would also like to thank Sun Lu Tang's daughter, Sun Jian Yun, for her patience and openness. While working on this book I met with Sun Jian Yun four times and each time she gladly answered all of my questions and provided me with written material on her father's life as well as photographs of her father.

Special thanks to Tim Cartmell, Xu Yu Hong, Huang Guo Qi, and Ren Jun for translating my interviews with Sun Jian Yun. Tim Cartmell, his wife Gu Feng Mei, and Huang Guo Qi also translated all of the written material on Sun Lu Tang's life provided by Sun Jian Yun and Sun Jian Yun's personal footnotes on her father's Xing Yi Quan book.

I would also like to thank my wife, Nancy Miller, for her patience, support, and proof-reading.

Forward to the English Translation

My father, Mr. Sun Lu Tang, a native of Wan County, Hebei Province, adored Chinese Martial Arts since his childhood. He studied Xing Yi Quan from Master Li Kui Yuan and then studied from Master Guo Yun Shen, and afterward studied Ba Gua Zhang from Master Cheng Ting Hua and Tai Ji Quan from Master Hao Wei Zhen.

After practicing for several dozens of years his skills became perfectly proficient. My father created Sun style Tai Ji Quan with a mixture of Xing Yi Quan, Ba Gua Quan, and Tai Ji Quan, therefore, it became a unique school of the arts.

My father spent his whole life in the research of martial arts and literature and wrote books to create new theories. His books are popular around the world.

My father was excellent in calligraphy and proficient in *Yi Jing*. My father had perfect personality and morality. His students are everywhere, at home and abroad. He was a true master of his generation.

Sun Jian Yun
Beijing Sun Style Tai Ji Quan
Association President
Beijing, China
September 1993

Sun Lu Tang
His Life and Teaching
by Dan Miller

孫祿堂大師

**Sun Lu Tang in 1929 at the Jiangsu
Province Martial Arts School**

Introduction

Today, almost anyone who practices the Chinese "internal" styles of martial arts can tell you that the arts of Ba Gua Zhang (八卦掌), Xing Yi Quan (形意拳), and Tai Ji Quan (太極拳) are the three most popular arts in the "internal" family and these arts are very good for health maintenance. They can also discourse, to some degree, about how these arts are related to Chinese philosophy and Daoism. However, in the late 1800's, when these arts were experiencing great popularity among the individuals who used these arts for fighting, there was not much talk of philosophy or health maintenance, nor was there a grouping of these styles into one family. Prior to the turn of the century the individuals who practiced these arts were primarily uneducated farmers who studied the arts in order to obtain jobs as bodyguards, residence guards and caravan escorts. The educated people in China looked down upon the martial artists and considered them low class ruffians. As Sun Lu Tang wrote in the preface to his Xing Yi Quan book, "There was a prejudice in the old days that literates despised martial arts as martial artists were short on literary learning."

The first known grouping of these arts under the name "internal family" occurred in 1894. Ba Gua Zhang master Cheng Ting Hua (程庭華) and his friends Liu De Kuan (劉德寬), Li Cun Yi (李存義), and Liu Wei Xiang (劉緯祥) came together to form an organization of martial artists in order to improve the level of their arts, increase harmony within the martial arts circles, and raise the skill level of their students. This "brotherhood" consisted of Cheng Ting Hua representing the Ba Gua school, Liu De Guan representing the Tai Ji school, and Li Cun Yi and Liu Wei Xiang representing the Xing Yi school. These teachers joined together and agreed that any students who studied with one of them, could freely study with the others. Through their collaboration these instructors improved their instructional techniques and decided that the three arts, although each having their own special points, were of the same "family."

In order to provide this martial arts family with a name, the group originally called it *Nei Jia Quan* (內家拳 - Internal Family Boxing). Later, after it was discovered that there had previously been an art called *Nei Jia Quan*, the name was changed to *Nei Gong Quan* (內功拳 - Internal Skill Boxing), however it was too late, the name *Nei Jia Quan* had stuck. This is how the arts of Ba Gua Zhang, Xing Yi Quan, and Tai Ji Quan became grouped together in the same family and why they are known as "internal" styles. The first publicly published works which referred to these arts being "internal" and of the same family were the books published by Sun Lu Tang (孫祿堂) in the early part of this century.

In the past, the arts of Ba Gua Zhang, Xing Yi Quan and Tai Ji Quan have also been grouped under the name "Wu Dang (武當) Boxing." This name has falsely led people to believe that these arts could trace their origins to the Daoists of Wu Dang mountain. The truth is that the origination of each of these arts can be clearly traced to places other than Wu Dang and, of the three, Ba Gua Zhang is the only one which evolved directly from specific Daoist practices. So, one might ask, were did the name "Wu Dang" come in?

During the Ming Dynasty there was a martial arts practitioner named Sun Shi San (孫十三) who practiced a boxing style which he called *Nei Jia Quan*. The first written record of this style appeared towards the end of the Ming Dynasty. A practitioner of *Nei Jia Quan* named Wang Zheng Nan (王征南) had a student, Huang Bai Jia (黃白家), who was the son of a famous scholar, Huang Zong Xi (黃宗義). When Wang Zheng Nan died, Huang Zong Xi wrote a eulogy for him which spoke of his boxing style and the events of his life. Huang Bai Jia subsequently took what his father had written about his teacher's boxing and published it in a book which he called *Nei Jia Quan*. In this book, which was published sometime during the late Ming or early Qing period, Huang Bai Jia wrote that this art had originated with the Daoist Zhang San Feng (張三丰) on Wu Dang mountain. Since the Chinese love to accredit famous historical and mythical figures with the origination of cultural arts and philosophy, Zhang San Feng is a questionable source for the origination of *Nei Jia Quan*. No clear lineage is given between Zhang San Feng and Wang Zhen Nan, so it is still unknown where the *Nei Jia Quan* of Wang's book originated.[1]

In 1894 when Cheng Ting Hua's group began associating the arts of Ba Gua Zhang, Xing Yi Quan, and Tai Ji Quan with the name *Nei Jia Quan*, people falsely assumed that these arts had some direct connection with the *Nei Jia Quan* of Huang Bai Jia's book. They further falsely assumed that these arts could trace their origins to the Daoists on Wu Dang mountain. The title "Wu Dang Boxing" was further lodged into the minds of practitioners when the Central Martial Arts Academy in Nanjing categorized these arts as "Wu Dang" styles in 1928 to distinguish them from the other styles which were of Shaolin (少林) origin. As mentioned above, the first individual who actually published material which connected the "internal" arts with Daoist principles was Sun Lu Tang. Others had undoubtedly made these connections, however, Sun was the first to write about it.

Sun Lu Tang was a rare breed in the martial arts circles at the turn of the century because he was a skilled martial artist and also had deep knowledge of the literary arts. After he had studied Ba Gua Zhang with Cheng Ting Hua, Cheng encouraged him to travel to Sichuan's E Mei mountain area and to Wu Dang mountain in order to investigate Daoism and the *Yi Jing* (易經 - *The Book of Changes*). Cheng associated with a number of scholars in Beijing and saw connections between the Daoist philosophy and the Ba Gua art. Recognizing that Sun was intelligent, he encouraged Sun to pursue the philosophy in order to deepen his understanding of the martial arts. Sun took Cheng's advice and traveled to E Mei and Wu Dang between 1894 and 1896. By the time Sun wrote his first book, *The Study of Form-Mind Boxing*, in 1915, he had studied Tai Ji, Xing Yi, and Ba Gua, and had also studied Daoist philosophy, the *Yi Jing* and Daoist longevity arts.

Sun Lu Tang's Xing Yi Quan book proved to be a turning point in the way the martial arts were viewed by the educated people in China and by the date this book was published, the time was ripe for this change. Around the turn of the century the Chinese people were generally very weak and of poor health. Bad crops, a corrupt government, and opium addiction had beaten the Chinese down. The foreigners living in China at the time gave the Chinese people the nickname "sick men of Asia." In an effort to strengthen the country, the new Republican government began introducing martial arts instruction in the schools and supported the practice of martial arts to improve health. One of the primary reasons Sun published his first book was to help promote martial arts for health. In his preface Sun wrote, "A strong country cannot be composed of weak people. We cannot make people strong without physical training. To brace up the people through physical training is the way to strengthen the country."

Sun Lu Tang's Xing Yi Quan book was the first book to be published publicly that grouped the arts of Xing Yi Quan, Ba Gua Zhang, and Tai Ji Quan in one family and it was the first written work to make a correspondence between martial arts, the *Yi Jing*, and Daoist philosophy. Thus this book helped mold our present day ideas about these arts.

---

1) This information is based on the research of Professor Kang Ge Wu of the Wushu Research Institute of China in Beijing. Professor Kang conducted this research while preparing a book on the history of Chinese martial arts which is soon to be released in China.

A Biography of Sun Lu Tang

The name Sun Lu Tang (孫祿堂) rings familiar to almost anyone who has studied one or more of the major "internal" styles of Chinese martial arts. Because Sun was highly skilled in Xing Yi Quan (形意拳), Tai Ji Quan (太極拳), and Ba Gua Zhang (八卦掌), wrote five different books on these subjects, and synthesized the three arts to invent Sun style Tai Ji Quan, his name has become well known wherever Chinese martial arts are practiced.

Like many of the Chinese martial arts heroes, as Sun's fame grew he became legendary and fantastic tales of his martial arts abilities spread like wildfire. Sun's daughter, Sun Jian Yun (孫劍雲), who is now over 80 years old, shakes her head when she hears many of the stories that are commonly told about her father. She states that although her father was a very highly skilled martial artist, he was not super-human. In a series of interviews conducted in Sun Jian Yun's home in Beijing, China, in October 1992 and September 1993, Sun Jian Yun discussed her father's background in detail and gave me the version of Sun Lu Tang's biography which she helped write and endorses as being true. The information in this chapter is primarily based on the book Sun Jian Yun gave to me and the interviews with Sun Jian Yun.

Sun's Childhood

Sun Lu Tang, also known as Sun Fu Quan (孫福全), was born in 1861 in Wan County, near the City of Bao Ding (保定), in Hebei (河北) Province. At that time in China's history the Qing government was very corrupt and as a result the Chinese common people were suffering. In Ju Li, Wan County, Sun Lu Tang's father had a small farm. Sun's father worked very hard but, because of the heavy taxes imposed by the Qing, he could barely scrape out a living as a farmer. He was middle aged and still unmarried when one of his friends, who knew that he was very honest and hard-working, acted as a matchmaker and introduced Sun's father to a young woman. Soon thereafter the two were married. A year after their marriage, in 1861 (4 January), they had a son who they named Fu Quan. This name was chosen because its meaning conveys that the baby would bring good fortune to their family.

An early photo (pre-1911) of Sun Lu Tang (1861-1933) taken at the home of Xu Shi Chang where Sun gave instruction

From a young age Sun Fu Quan was very intelligent. Recognizing the boy's intellectual abilities, his father sent him to study with a local scholar when he was seven years old. Because Sun's father did not have a lot of money, he gave the scholar food from his field in exchange for teaching his son. Sun Fu Quan was an exceptionally bright student. By the time he was nine he had already read and memorized many of the classical text such as the *Three Character Classic* (*San Zi Jing* 三字經) and various Confucian works. Memorization of these classics through repetitive speaking and writing was the main curriculum of study for students of the time. Sun's memory was exceptional and by the time he was nine he had already memorized many of the texts and was also proficient at the basic calligraphy strokes.

The year Sun turned nine his father did not have a good harvest and therefore he could not afford to pay the very high taxes which the Qing government imposed on the people. Because of the poor harvest, Sun's father could not afford to pay his tutor, so Sun did not continue with his formal education. The situation became so desperate that in order to avoid going to jail, Sun's father sold everything he owned, including his land, to pay his taxes. Shortly after he sold his land, the elder Sun became ill and died. Consequently, Sun and his mother were left with no land and no income. They could not even afford a casket in which to bury his father and so his father's body lay in the house for three days before Sun begged enough money for a casket.

With no land to farm and no other means of support, Sun's mother did not feel as though she could raise her son. She went to a rich and powerful local landowner and asked if he would take her son as a servant. He reluctantly agreed saying that he would let Sun live at his home and he would feed him, but he would not give him any money because Sun was so small and frail looking. He did not think the boy could do enough work to earn a salary on top of room and board. Sun's new employer had a son, two years older than Sun, who took pleasure in bullying Sun. In addition, Sun's employer took any opportunity he could to beat him. Sun wanted to fight back, but he knew that if he lost his job he would not be able to take care of himself and his mother would be upset. He worked as hard as he could and silently endured the beatings when they came.

Sun Discovers Martial Arts

One day Sun was out in a field tending to sheep when he heard people yelling. He climbed up on a nearby hill and saw a group practicing martial arts. The teacher was a man about 70 years old with an average build. He had a lot of spirit in his eyes and when he demonstrated his art his movements were quick, crisp, and clear. Sun had never seen martial arts before and was fascinated with what he saw. He decided that the next day he would find this teacher and ask to be taught martial arts.

The next day Sun found the teacher's house and knelt before him to ask permission to become a student. At first the teacher thought that Sun was kidding. He asked where Sun was from and Sun told the teacher the story about how his father had died and that he worked for a man who beat him. The teacher was moved by Sun's honesty and sincerity. He asked why Sun wanted to study martial arts. Sun replied that he wanted to fight back when his employer and employer's son beat on him. The old man said, "Martial arts are not only for fighting, these principles are very deep." Sun was adamant about studying. The teacher asked if he could stand the hardship of it and

Sun replied that he could stand any kind of suffering as long as he could study martial arts. The teacher, whose surname was Wu, agreed to accept Sun as a student.

Sun was ten years old when he began studying with his first martial arts instructor. Every day after work he would go and study until the middle of the night. His teacher had also had a very hard life as a youngster and sympathized with Sun's situation. After becoming skilled in martial arts, Wu was very righteous and helped oppressed people. On one occasion he came to someone's aid who was being beaten and subsequently killed the attacker. The government wanted to execute him for this crime and so he fled his home. To make a living he performed his martial arts in the streets and begged for money. Later he joined the Tai Ping Rebellion (1850-1864) and fought against the Qing soldiers. After the Tai Ping dispersed, he went back to performing martial arts in the streets for money. He was an expert at *Shaolin* (少林) and *Ba Ji Quan* (八極拳) as well as the eighteen weapons. He was also skilled at shooting iron balls from a sling shot and had *qing gong* (輕功), or lightness skill.

Sun Lu Tang was an exceptional student. After the first year of practice he had become proficient at the basic skills and began studying *Hong Quan* (洪拳). Sun also studied the 64 hands free fighting method, lightness skill, "virgin boy" *qi gong* (氣功), and hidden weapons skills. Wu recognized Sun's natural skill and intelligence and therefore taught him at a rapid pace. After two years of study, Sun was the best boxer of his age in the area. So that Sun would not become too cocky, his teacher reminded him that although he was progressing quickly, he had still only touched the surface of real martial arts and therefore he should not become overly proud of what he had achieved. His teacher told him a story of when he himself was young and had attained a good level of skill for his age. He thought he was very good and went to someone's aid who was getting beat up. The opponent who he fought was a highly skilled martial artist and injured him badly. Wu said that his opponent would have killed him had not a Shaolin monk been there witnessing the fight and intervened in order to save him before it was too late. The monk took Wu back to the Shaolin temple and he stayed there for two years studying. At the temple he studied *tan tui* (彈腿), the 64 hands free fighting, the 72 *qin na* (擒拿), and *qing gong*.

After Sun had been with his teacher for three years, his mother heard that he was practicing martial arts. This made her very nervous because she thought he was too frail and might get hurt. She went to see him with the intention of telling him not to practice anymore.

However, when she arrived she saw that he was much stronger and healthier than he had been before and so she did not try to stop him from practicing. Sun had always been thin and weak and upon seeing her son's physical improvement she realized that the martial arts were good for him.

When Sun was approximately 12 years old, his boss let all of the servants have half a day off to celebrate the new year. Sun had planned to go home and visit with his mother. As he was about to leave, the boss' son came in and started pushing Sun around. He said, "You have been practicing martial arts! If you think you are good, let us see you fight with my cousin." The cousin, who was 8 years older than Sun, came into the room. He was a very big, strong looking practitioner of Chinese Wrestling (*Shuai Jiao* 摔角). The cousin grabbed Sun by the shirt and dragged him into the courtyard. Once in the courtyard, the aggressor grabbed Sun by the pants and shirt, picked him up over his head and threw him. When he was thrown, Sun flipped over in the air and landed on his feet. This made the cousin mad, however, Sun was also angry because his shirt had been ripped. As Sun's opponent ran over to pick him up and throw him again, Sun punched him in the solar plexus and knocked him on his back. When he hit the ground, the cousin vomited all of the new year's food he had just consumed. Sun's boss' son ran and got his father. Sun's boss came out in the courtyard with a big stick and said he was going to beat Sun to death. The other servants held the boss back and tried to convince him not to beat Sun. The boss yelled at Sun to leave and never come back or else he would beat him to death. Sun left and went home to his mother.

The only thing that interested the young Sun Fu Quan was the martial arts. He did not want to work, he only wanted to study. To feed himself, and ease the burden on his mother, he would eat wild vegetables that he found. Because many martial artists of the day had bad reputations, the local villagers thought that he would surely grow up to be a bandit. This made him even more determined. He told them that not only was he going to be a great martial artist, but one day he would help this village and make all of the villagers proud.

Shortly after being fired from his job, Sun became very ashamed and depressed because he could not take care of his mother and he could not keep a job. One day he told his mother that he was going to go beg for some rice. Sun felt so depressed that instead of begging for rice, he went out and hung himself. Immediately after he had drawn the noose tight around his neck, two traveler's came by and cut him down. Sun was not yet dead so they took him back home to his mother. The two kind-hearted travelers talked with Sun and convinced him that no matter how bad the circumstances, he should not try to kill himself. One of the travelers gave Sun and his mother some money and they used it to go to Bao Ding to visit Sun's uncle.

Sun's uncle owned a shop where he sold calligraphy brushes. He gave Sun a job working as a clerk in the shop. While working in his Uncle's shop, Sun practiced his calligraphy every day. He was too poor to buy paper or ink and so he would use scrap paper and write on it with water. Sun's Uncle was a kind man and his shop was very successful. In addition to room and board for Sun and his mother, his Uncle would periodically give Sun money for working in the shop. It was through his Uncle's connections that Sun was able to continue his martial arts practice in Bao Ding. Sun's Uncle had two very close friends. One friend, surnamed Zhang, was a scholar and the other, named Li Kui Yuan (李魁元), was a martial artist who owned the *Tai An* bodyguard service.

Li Kui Yuan had been a Xing Yi Quan student of the famous Guo Yun Shen (郭雲深). He had met Guo one day when he was on a job escorting a convoy. On this occasion, he challenged Guo to a friendly match so that he could test his own skill. Li was famous for his legwork and kicking techniques. During the match, Li tried to kick Guo. Guo blocked the kick with what appeared to be a light tap, however, Li flew back several yards and fell on the ground. When Li got up he was not hurt. Because Guo had met the challenge and defeated him soundly without hurting him, Li knew he had run into a very high level martial artist. He ran over to Guo, knelt down and asked to become a student. Guo agreed to teach him and Li began studying Xing Yi Quan with Guo. Li studied Xing Yi Quan with Guo for several years. Since Li was already skilled in martial arts, Guo taught him quickly and thus he greatly improved his martial arts abilities. After studying with Guo, Li earned the nickname "divine skill" Li.

One day Sun Lu Tang's Uncle was preparing to send a gift to his scholar friend Zhang and asked Sun to write the name and address on the package. When Zhang received the gift he was more impressed with the calligraphy on the package than he was with the gift which was inside. Zhang went to visit Sun's Uncle to ask who had written the calligraphy. When he found out that it was his friend's nephew who had written the calligraphy, Zhang said, "You never told me you had a young man in your family with such talent." Zhang told Sun, who was about 15 at the time, that he could come to his home as often as he would like and learn more about calligraphy. During his spare time Sun began to go to Zhang's house to practice. It was there that he first met the martial artist Li Kui Yuan. Upon meeting Sun, Li found him to be an upright and intelligent boy. Learning that Sun had a background in martial arts, Li offered to teach him Xing Yi Quan. Sun's love for martial arts had not faded and he was thrilled to have found a new instructor.

Sun Studies Xing Yi Quan

For the first year Sun studied Xing Yi Quan with Li he was only taught the *San Ti* (三 體) standing posture. He was not allowed to practice anything else. Sun wondered why he was taught only standing, however, since his teacher had told him to only practice standing, he did not complain. After about six months, Sun started to feel as though his chest and stomach were full and his feet had roots. He was starting to develop internal power from his standing practice and he figured that this is what real *gong fu* (功 夫) was all about. After these experiences he started to stand more diligently. After Sun had practiced standing for approximately one year, his teacher saw him practicing one day and snuck up on him to test his level. Li hit Sun on his back with a palm strike and Sun's standing posture was not affected by the blow. He realized that Sun had attained a good level of development and had great potential so he invited Sun to come live with him and started to teach him Xing Yi Quan's five elements and twelve animals. Sun practiced his Xing Yi Quan so hard that after only two years of training he had developed a much higher level of Xing Yi Quan skill than was expected of someone of his age and experience.

On the scholar Zhang's fiftieth birthday Li and Sun went to his home to wish him well. On this occasion, Zhang suggested that Li accept Sun as his formal disciple. Li agreed that Sun had studied hard enough to earn a place in his Xing Yi Quan lineage and accepted Sun as a seventh generation disciple of his branch of Xing Yi Quan. This branch of Xing Yi Quan originated with Ji Ji Ke (姬 際 可 - also known as Ji Long Feng 姬 隆 風) and was passed to Cao Ji Wu (曹 繼 武), then to Dai Long Bang (戴 隆 邦), to Li Neng Ran (李 能 然), to Guo Yun Shen, to Li Kui Yuan, and then to Sun Lu Tang.

After Zhang had made the suggestion that Li accept Sun as a disciple, Li made a suggestion to Zhang. He said, "Now that I have accepted a formal disciple at your encouragement, I will encourage you to accept a son-in-law and allow Sun to marry your daughter." Zhang's daughter, Zhang Zhao Xien (張 昭 賢), was 16 years old at the time and Sun was about 18. Zhang and Li thought that the two would make a good match and so they became engaged. However, Sun did not want to marry right away. He wanted to spend more time practicing martial arts before he had to worry about supporting his wife.

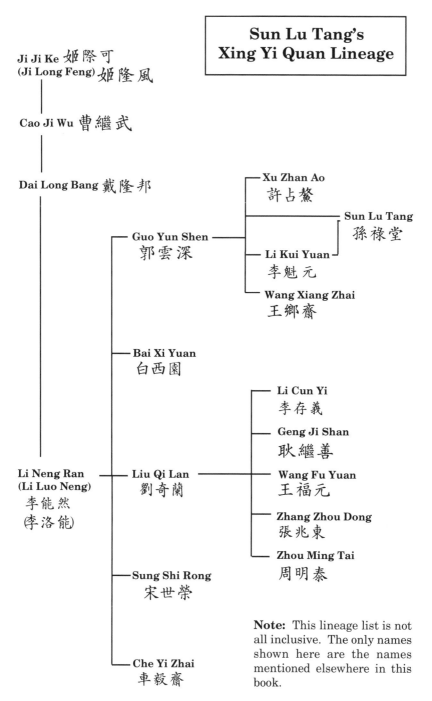

Sun Lu Tang's Xing Yi Quan Lineage

Ji Ji Ke 姬際可
(Ji Long Feng) 姬隆風

Cao Ji Wu 曹繼武

Dai Long Bang 戴隆邦

Li Neng Ran
(Li Luo Neng)
李能然
(李洛能)

Guo Yun Shen
郭雲深

Xu Zhan Ao
許占鰲

Li Kui Yuan
李魁元

Sun Lu Tang
孫祿堂

Wang Xiang Zhai
王鄉齋

Bai Xi Yuan
白西園

Liu Qi Lan
劉奇蘭

Li Cun Yi
李存義

Geng Ji Shan
耿繼善

Wang Fu Yuan
王福元

Zhang Zhou Dong
張兆東

Zhou Ming Tai
周明泰

Sung Shi Rong
宋世榮

Che Yi Zhai
車毅齋

Note: This lineage list is not all inclusive. The only names shown here are the names mentioned elsewhere in this book.

12

A group of Qing Dynasty era Xing Yi Quan practitioners. Guo Yun Shen is seated wearing the white robe and black vest.

Li Kui Yuan told Sun that he had taught him just about everything that he knew. He suggested that if Sun wanted to learn more about Xing Yi Quan he would introduce him to his teacher, Guo Yun Shen. Sun was very excited about the possibility of studying with Guo, but he was a little worried about someone taking care of his mother. Zhang the scholar told Sun not to worry about it. He said that he would take Sun's mother into his house and look after her while Sun was studying with Guo. With his mother taken care of, Sun was ready to go continue pursuing his martial arts study. Li took Sun to Shen County in Hebei Province to introduce him to his teacher Guo Yun Shen.

Guo Yun Shen had studied Xing Yi Quan with Li Neng Ran (also known as Li Luo Neng). Guo loved to fight when he was young. When he first approached Li Neng Ran wanting to learn Xing Yi Quan, Li would not teach him because he was of such a violent nature. Li told Guo that unless he could change his character, he would never teach him martial arts. Guo got a job as a servant near Li's home and would secretly watch Li and his students practice Xing Yi. Guo practiced *Beng quan* (崩拳 - smashing fist) on his own for three years. One day Li Neng Ran saw Guo practicing *beng quan* and noticed that Guo was very good at it already. Li realized that Guo was sincere about learning Xing Yi Quan so he then agreed to teach him.

After Guo had studied with Li for a few years he got a job as a bounty hunter. The law of the day said that a bounty hunter was allowed to catch criminals and bring them in, however, the criminals had to be brought in alive. On one occasion, Guo was hunting a bandit who was terrorizing travelers along a frequently traveled road. Guo found the bandit he was pursuing while the bandit was engaged in a fight with a local escort service. Guo joined the battle and captured the bandit, however, after he had captured him, the bandit pulled out a concealed weapon and tried to kill Guo. Guo hit the man and killed him. Recognizing that he had done wrong, Guo turned himself in to the authorities. The penalty for such a crime was death, however, the local magistrate's advisors begged him to consider not executing Guo because he was a rare talent in the martial arts. Instead of execution, the magistrate sentenced Guo to three years in prison. While in prison Guo was manacled, however, he continued to practice his Xing Yi Quan. When he came out of prison his skill was higher than when he had entered.

While in prison, Guo had developed what became known as *ban bu beng quan* (半步崩拳 - half step smashing fist) and became so famous for the power he developed with this special punch that people said that his "half step smashing fist could beat all under heaven." After being released from prison, Guo went to visit the escort service

14

doing business in the area where the bandit he had killed had operated. He told them that ever since he had killed the bandit, the road was clear and their job had become easy. He told the escort service that they owed him money because of the work he had done for them. Because of his martial arts skill, they did not want to quarrel with him so they gave him some money. However, Guo would periodically come back for more money and the escort service got tired of it. Instead of confronting Guo directly, they sent a letter to Guo's teacher Li Neng Ran.

Guo Yun Shen's elder Xing Yi brother Che Yi Zhai

Li Neng Ran called Guo back home and told him that he shouldn't bother the escort service any more. Li also said, "Plus, your *gong fu* is not nearly as good as you think it is. Your skill does not come close to that of your older brother Che Yi Zhai (車毅齋)." In telling Guo this, Li wanted to teach him two lessons. The first was that he should not be so arrogant because no matter how good someone gets, there is always someone better. The second reason was to try and bring him back to complete his Xing Yi training. After Guo learned the five fists of Xing Yi, he did not want to study anything else. He was so good at applying the five fists that he never lost a fight, therefore, he concluded that he did not need to learn anything else. Li had encouraged Guo to study Xing Yi Quan's subsequent forms and two-person sets after he had learned the five fists, but Guo thought it was a bother and left Li before his Xing Yi training was complete.

Upon hearing that his teacher thought that Che Yi Zhai's skill was better than his, Guo became angry and went to Shanxi Province to find Che Yi Zhai and challenge him. When Guo arrived at Che's home, Che was happy to see him and said "Little brother, I am glad you have come to visit! Let's have something to eat." Guo said, "No, I came here to fight." Che tried to talk Guo out of fighting, but Guo persisted and thus Che was left without a choice. Guo tried to use his famous *beng quan* over and over. Che kept backing away from Guo's strikes and then quickly turned to the side as Guo struck again and executed *pi quan* (劈拳 - splitting fist). Che held the strike, stopping inches from Guo's head. Realizing that Che had got the best of him, Guo stopped and said, "It is just as our teacher has said, you are better then I." Following this incident Guo never bothered the escort company again and he went back to Li Neng Ran in order to complete his Xing Yi training.

Sun Lu Tang meets Guo Yun Shen

Li Kui Yuan had already been middle aged by the time he had begun studying with Guo Yun Shen and although his skill level was very high, he had never reached the level of his teacher. When Li took Sun Lu Tang to Ma Village in Shen County to meet Guo in the Spring of 1882, Guo accepted Sun as a student and Li also stayed to continue his practice with Guo. Sun moved in with his new teacher and studied Xing Yi Quan full time. When Guo saw Sun's Xing Yi Quan he was very impressed. He said that Sun was especially skilled in Xing Yi's monkey form and so he nicknamed Sun "living monkey." It is said that Sun had so much natural talent he eventually surpassed the level of his original teacher, Li Kui Yuan.

During the first year of practice, Guo did not teach Sun much new material but watched him practice what he already knew and made corrections. One night, after Sun had been there for about a year, he was outside practicing when Guo leapt out of the shadows and tried to attack him with *beng quan* (smashing fist). Sun instinctively used a leaping move from the monkey form and leapt back about ten feet. Guo was very happy that Sun could react so well and from that time forward began to teach him deeply.

Guo Yun Shen ran a farm and supported Sun while Sun studied with him. Sun traveled with Guo everywhere he went. Guo often traveled long distances on horseback. In order to develop Sun's stamina and strength, Guo required him to walk along beside the horse with his arm held straight out behind the horse with the horse's tail draped over his arm. Sun was required to keep the arm held out and always travel at the same pace as the horse by keeping the tail draped over the arm. One version of this story says that Sun was able to keep up with the horse even when the horse was running. When Sun's daughter, Sun Jian Yun, was asked about this story, she said, "That is ridiculous, no man could run as fast as a horse!" The distances Sun traveled while following the horse and the speed at which he could run have been greatly exaggerated in books and articles written about Sun.

Later, Guo gave Sun the book of Xing Yi Quan that he had received from his teacher Li Neng Ran. Sun knelt down and accepted the book and said that he would always strive to represent the system with honor. Sun then became the formal inheritor of Guo Yun Shen's Xing Yi Quan. Altogether Sun stayed with Guo for eight years at which time Guo told Sun that if he wanted to add a new dimension to his martial arts he should practice Ba Gua Zhang to become skilled at evasiveness. Guo told Sun he would like to take him to Beijing to study Ba Gua Zhang with his friend Cheng Ting Hua. The year was 1889.

Guo Yun Shen and Cheng Ting Hua were both natives of Shen County in Hebei. Shen County lies in south-central Hebei, south of Bao Ding and west of Hebei's capital city, Shi Jia Zhuang. The natives of Shen County were, and still are, primarily farmers. However, because of its central location in Hebei, there were many frequently traveled roads running through Shen County. During the Qing Dynasty, and even into the Republican period, police protection was only provided to those people who lived in the large cities. Consequently, the people who traveled the roads in Shen and the surrounding rural counties had little protection against the bandits and thieves who frequented the area. Many skilled martial artists set up bodyguard, or caravan guard services in areas like Shen County and hired themselves out to protect travelers against the bandits. Needless to say, the martial artists in this area of Hebei were highly skilled. Li Lou Neng, Guo Yun Shen, Cheng Ting Hua, Liu Qi Lan, Li Cun Yi, Wang Fu Yuan, Geng Ji Shan and Wang Xiang Zhai were all natives of Shen county and this is where Sun Lu Tang studied his Xing Yi Quan with Guo Yun Shen.

Since Guo Yun Shen and Cheng Ting Hua were both natives of the same county, they probably knew each other before Cheng went to Beijing and studied Ba Gua Zhang with the system's originator, Dong Hai Quan (董海川). Even if they hadn't known each other personally, they would have certainly known each other by reputation. In any event the story about how they became close friends is an interesting one. During the late 1800's Ba Gua Zhang was becoming quite popular in Beijing and its originator, Dong Hai Chuan was famous. Guo, who was famous in his own right for his Xing Yi Quan skill, wanted to go to Beijing and test Dong abilities.

When Guo arrived in Beijing, he went to visit Cheng Ting Hua first. Since they were from the same county, Cheng invited Guo to stay with him. When Cheng asked Guo the purpose of his trip to Beijing, Guo told Cheng about his plan to challenge Dong and asked what Cheng thought about it. Cheng knew of Guo's great Xing Yi Quan skill, however, he advised Guo against challenging Dong because Dong had never been beaten. Guo faced Cheng and said, "Brother, how about if you suffer my *beng quan*?" That was all the notification

Cheng got that the punch was coming. Cheng quickly dodged the punch and Guo's incoming fist struck a door frame, knocking a piece of it off. Guo was startled at Cheng's speed and agility and knew that Dong was much better than Cheng, so he dropped the idea of a challenge with Dong Hai Quan. Guo and Cheng held mutual respect for each other's martial art and agreed that top students from each system should study the other in order to refine their skills. Consequently, after Sun Lu Tang had become skilled in Xing Yi Quan, Guo took him to Cheng Ting Hua to learn Ba Gua Zhang.

Some accounts of the story of Guo Yun Shen coming to challenge Dong Hai Chuan say that Dong and Guo actually did fight. In this story Guo and Dong fought for three days. For the first two days Guo could not penetrate Dong's circular defense, on the third day Dong took the offensive and humbled Guo without actually hurting him. The two were so impressed with the other's skill that they made a pact that practitioners of each system would train in the other. The majority of boxing masters from both the Ba Gua Zhang and Xing Yi Quan schools in Hebei Province and the martial arts scholars in mainland China say that there is no truth to this fable. Dong Hai Chuan and Guo Yun Shen never fought each other.

Sun Begins his Study of Ba Gua Zhang

Sun Lu Tang was very interested in going to Beijing to study with Cheng Ting Hua, but first he went back to Bao Ding to visit his mother and tell the scholar Zhang and his daughter that he would like to put the wedding off for a little while longer. He received their permission and set off for Beijing to study with Cheng. Cheng accepted Sun as a student and began teaching him Ba Gua Zhang. Sun Lu Tang was almost 30 years old at the time. Cheng began teaching Sun Ba Gua Zhang by introducing him to the circle-walk practice.

After Sun had been practicing for a while, Cheng said that he was going to show Sun something about Ba Gua Zhang's fighting method. He asked Sun to attack him and not hold back. Sun attacked with *beng quan*. Cheng used Ba Gua Zhang's evasive footwork to quickly move out of the way of the attack and instantaneously positioned himself behind Sun. Sun continued attacking, however, every time he moved toward Cheng, Cheng would end up behind him. Finally, Sun turned one time and met Cheng's "double crashing palm" and was thrown back several yards. Sun was very impressed with Cheng and was disappointed with his own level of skill. Cheng told Sun that what he had used was only basic Ba Gua Zhang skills; the art of Ba Gua Zhang was much deeper than he had shown.

Liang Ke Quan (梁克權), a Xing Yi and Ba Gua instructor in Beijing

Sun Lu Tang with a group of Xing Yi Boxers in
Shanxi Province in 1924

 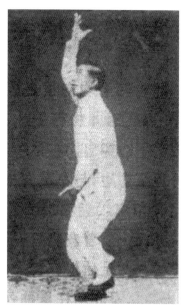

Photographs of Sun Lu Tang taken from his book
The Study of Ba Gua Boxing

who studied Ba Gua Zhang with Cheng Ting Hua's son Cheng You Xin (程有信), tells a story about Sun's early days with Cheng. Liang states that for the first year of study with Cheng the only thing Sun was allowed to practice was a few standing postures and walking the circle. However, he would practice other things on his own behind his teacher's back. There was an area behind the Forbidden City where some old cannons lay. Sun would practice hitting these cannons everyday and after several months of practice he could hit the cannons and make them move slightly even though they weighed several hundred pounds apiece.

After Sun had been with Cheng for almost a year, a famous martial artist came to Beijing from southern China to challenge Cheng Ting Hua. Cheng sent his best students out to fight the Southerner and all of Cheng's students were defeated. Cheng became nervous that he would lose his reputation, so he went to fight the guy himself. As he was leaving, Sun grabbed him and said, "I'll go fight him." Cheng said, "But all you have practiced is walking the circle, how can you expect to beat this man who has defeated my senior students?" Sun said, "He has beaten everyone else, so if he beats me, it is not much different, however, if he beats you, your reputation will be lost."

Cheng went to see the Southerner and told him that he had one more student to fight and Sun stepped forward. When the fight began Sun moved around the challenger and then quickly hit him like he had been hitting the cannons behind the Forbidden City. Sun hit him so hard that he knocked the man out of the window of the building. Cheng Ting Hua was so happy that he slapped the bench he was sitting on and broke it in half. The Southern martial artist knelt before Cheng and said, "The South has lost to the great Cheng Ting Hua."

Sun took notes on all that Cheng told him and this formed the basis of his later writing on Ba Gua Zhang. After studying with Cheng for three years Sun was proficient in the Ba Gua bare hand methods, Ba Gua sword, and Ba Gua spear. Cheng told him he had learned quickly because of his background and natural ability and gave Sun the nickname "More Clever Than An Active Monkey." After Sun had finished his three years of study with Cheng, Cheng told him that staying there longer was not going to help him much. Cheng said, "I have instructed over one hundred people. None of my other students is as intelligent or has practiced as hard as Sun. I have passed to him all of my skills and now his skill is invincible in this world."

Cheng told Sun that he needed to go test himself in the world. Sun was reluctant to leave, but Cheng told him he should go. Cheng told Sun that his *gong fu* skill was such that if he got into a fight, his teacher would not "loose face" and said, "The boxing skills of our school are closely related with the theory of the *Yi Jing*. If you want to climb the holy platform, it is necessary for you to study the origin and understand the theory of the *Yi Jing*. I know that some people in Sichuan Province are especially skilled in these theories. You should travel there." Before Sun left, Cheng said to remember this, "Pride will cause you harm while you will always benefit from humility." Cheng then gave him the name "Lu Tang." From then on in martial circles he was known as Sun Lu Tang.

Sun Jian Yun speaks of at least one instance where Sun's change of name caused some confusion later in his life. One of Cheng Ting Hua's other Ba Gua Zhang students, Zhou Yu Xiang (周玉祥) was teaching Ba Gua Zhang and Xing Yi Quan in Tianjin (Zhou had studied Xing Yi Quan with Li Cun Yi). Sun was in town and went by to visit Zhou. Although they were from the same Ba Gua Chang school, they had not studied with Cheng at the same time and thus they had never met. When Sun entered Zhou's school, Zhou asked his name and Sun replied, "I am Sun Lu Tang." Zhou had never heard of Sun Lu Tang, he had only ever heard of Sun Fu Quan, and so he did not know who this visitor was. Zhou asked Sun if he practiced martial arts. Sun, realizing that Zhou did not know who he was, said, "Yes, I practice

**Sun Lu Tang's friend
Ma Yu Tang**

Shaolin."

When Zhou heard that this visitor was a Shaolin practitioner his attitude conveyed that he thought his style superior to what the visitor practiced. He said, "Why don't you show me some of your Shaolin." Zhou attacked Sun in a friendly manner so Sun could apply his art. Sun performed an application. In response Zhou said, "That does not look like Shaolin to me. Let's try again." This time Zhou attacked with more force, trying to really hit him. Sun avoided the strike and struck Zhou in such a manner that Zhou's head went through the low paper ceiling. Zhou said, "That is not Shaolin. I recognize this as Xing Yi Quan. Who are you?" Sun replied, "As I have told you, I am Sun Lu Tang, also known as Sun Fu Quan." Zhou said, "Now I know who you are. We are boxing brothers! Why didn't you tell me?" Zhou then apologized for his rudeness.

A similar friendly encounter occurred between Sun and another of Li Cun Yi's students, Ma Yu Tang (馬玉堂). Sun was working as a bodyguard for a government official in Xing Tang City in Hebei. Sun and Ma knew each other by name, but had never met each other. Ma Yu Tang was known for being somewhat of a practical joker. Ma was visiting the area where Sun lived and was hoping to meet him. He was out one evening and recognized the government official who was known to be Sun's employer. Although Ma did not know what Sun looked like, he figured that the man traveling with the government official must be Sun Lu Tang. When the official entered a small building Sun waited outside in the narrow alley. Ma came up behind Sun and leapt at him in mock-attack. Sun quickly turned and grabbed Ma in such a manner that Ma could not move. Sun Shouted, "Who are you!" Ma replied, "I am Ma Yu Tang. We are from the same system of Xing Yi Quan." Sun said, "Yes, I have heard of you and I knew that it must have been you attacking me in such a manner. You are the only one crazy enough to do such a thing!" They both laughed and became good friends.

Sun Lu Tang Goes Out On His Own

After Sun Lu Tang left Cheng Ting Hua at the end of 1891, he could not take his teacher's advice and travel to Sichuan Province right away. He first returned to his hometown and married Zhang Shou Xin who had been patiently waiting for him. Sun took his new bride to Ding Xing County in Hebei Province and began teaching martial arts. When he first started teaching he was in his thirties. Many of the farmers in the area and other townspeople studied martial arts with him. Sun stayed there teaching for about three years and his wife gave birth to his first son, Sun Xing Yi (孫星一).

In 1894, Sun followed the advice of Cheng Ting Hua and traveled to Sichuan Province. While in Sichuan he met a monk named Zhi Zhen (知貞) and studied *Yi Jing* theory and *E Mei qi gong* (峨眉氣功). After a short stay in Sichuan, Sun traveled to Wu Dang mountain in Hubei Province. At Wu Dang, Sun studied the "immortality skill" of Daoism with the chief Daoist at the temple, Jing Xu (靜虛). The Daoist wanted Sun to stay at the temple indefinitely and continue studying, however,

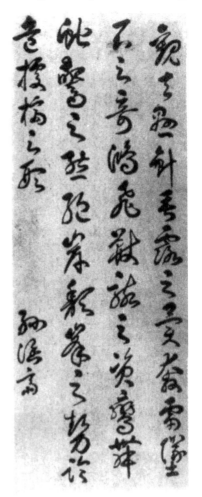

Sun Lu Tang's calligraphy

after he had been away from home for two years, Sun returned to his wife and child. While on his trip to Sichuan and Hubei, Sun's skills became more perfect and his literary intelligence was greatly enhanced.

Sun returned to his wife in 1896 and they moved to his hometown near Bao Ding. When he arrived, Sun established the Pu Yang Boxing Association. Sun taught many students and entertained visitors from all walks of life.

One of Sun's best students in Bao Ding was named Qi Gong Bo (齊公博). When Qi started studying Xing Yi Quan with Sun, he did nothing for three years but stand in the *San Ti* posture. Many Xing Yi

Sun Lu Tang as an Army Officer, circa 1920

Quan masters in China recommend that if one wants to become skilled in Xing Yi Quan, they spend a lot of time standing in the *San Ti* posture. This was a requirement in the old days. If one travels to Bao Ding today they can see Sun's martial arts still being practiced by many of the martial artists there. While teaching martial arts in his hometown, Sun also started a literary study society because most of the townspeople were illiterate.

After Sun left his hometown, around 1899, he traveled to Xing Tang, a town about 80 miles from Beijing in Hebei Province. Sun taught martial arts there for approximately eight years. On one occasion a wealthy land owner held a party. Sun was in attendance and the wealthy man was showing off his horse-riding skill. Knowing Sun was a famous martial artist, upon finishing a ride around the stable yard, the man asked Sun if he could ride a horse. Sun said, "You take one more ride and then I'll give it a try." The man rode the horse around the stable yard once more, demonstrating his best maneuvers so as to show up Sun. He finished his round to thunderous applause from the guests. Bowing proudly to the crowd, convinced that Sun could not perform near as well, the man looked to where Sun had been standing, but no one was there. He then realized that Sun was sitting on the horse behind him. Sun had been sitting there the during the entire demonstration and the applause from the crowd had been for Sun, not the land owner.

While Sun was living in Xing Tang there was a famous bandit nicknamed the "flying thief" because of his *qing gong* (lightness skill). The mayor of Xing Tang approached Sun and asked if he could help catch the bandit. Sun disguised himself as a fortune teller in the center of town and waited. When the thief appeared, Sun ran after him and the thief fled. One the edge of town there was a field full of a tall plants which are known for their very thick stalk. When the plant tops were removed during harvest, only the thick stalk remained. The "flying thief" ran to the field and leapt up on top of the densely planted crop and ran across the plant stalk tops. The thief was sure that no one could follow him, however when he turned around, he saw Sun still in pursuit, also running across the plant stalk tops. Sun caught the thief and turned him in.

One of the common practice methods in *qing gong* training is to learn how to maneuver quickly while stepping in patterns on top of thin wooden

Sun Lu Tang's Tai Ji teacher Hao Wei Zhen

posts which are driven into the ground. Evidently this training served Sun well in the apprehension of the bandit. Sun Jian Yun states that not only did her father have *qing gong* training when he was young and practicing Shaolin, but both the Ba Gua Zhang and Xing Yi Quan her father had practiced included *qing gong* training as well. She said that one of the developmental skills was to run as fast as one could up a slightly inclined ramp. Gradually one would increase the steepness of the incline until it was vertical. She said her father could run up a 10 foot wall in three steps, quickly turn around when he reached the ceiling and jump back down. She says that although there have been reports that he could stick to the ceiling when he ran up there, this was not true.

In 1907, Xu Shi Chang (徐世昌), the general governor of the three Northern provinces, heard about Sun's martial arts skill and intelligence and, in the name of spreading the national arts, he invited Sun to Northern China to teach. Sun took his younger school brother Li Wen Biao (李文彪), who had been a student of Li Cun Yi, and traveled North to Feng Tian to answer the governor's invitation. Soon after Sun arrived he defeated a bandit nicknamed "Invincible in the Eastern Provinces" and his reputation spread in the Northeastern areas of China. The second year he was there, Sun was prepared to enter a platform boxing match against a European. However, Xu thought if Sun won it would upset the foreigners so he called off the match.

Photographs of Sun Lu Tang taken from his book
The Study of Tai Ji Boxing

Later that year Sun left the Northeast and returned to his hometown.

In 1910, Sun decided that if he was going to promote the spread of martial arts in China, he could not do it from his small hometown and so he moved to Beijing and stayed there for the majority of his remaining years. He rented a house in the eastern part of the city and set up three martial arts training halls. Two of the schools were in Beijing and one was in Tianjin. The schools were administered by his school brother Li Wen Biao and one of his senior students, Li Yu Lin (李玉琳). Sun traveled between Beijing and Tianjin to accept new students and teach.

Sun also made a number of short trips to teach at the request of different martial arts schools around the country, however, he kept his home in Beijing until the month before he died when he returned to his hometown. When he moved to Beijing, Sun was about 48 years old. Sun Lu Tang's daughter, Sun Jian Yun was born on July 6, 1914, when Sun was 53.

While in Beijing, in the Summer of 1914, Sun heard that the famous Tai Ji Quan teacher Hao Wei Zhen (郝為貞) was there to visit his friend Yang Jian Hou (楊建侯). Evidently Hao could not locate Yang and had checked into an Inn and was subsequently taken ill. Sun went and got Hao Wei Zhen out of the Inn and brought Hao to his home. Sun brought a doctor to the house to look at Hao, went to get medicine for him and took care of him while he was sick. Up to this point Sun did not know that Hao practiced Tai Ji, he only knew that Hao was a famous martial artist. After Hao recovered from his illness, he told Sun that he would repay his kindness by teaching Sun his martial art. This is how Sun learned the Hao Style Tai Ji Quan from Hao Wei Zhen.

In July, 1915, Sun Lu Tang's first book, *The Study of Form-Mind Boxing* was published. It was the first book in the history of Chinese martial arts which explained the theory of the martial arts in relation to Chinese philosophy. There had

Sun Lu Tang's friend and student Chen Wei Ming

been numerous books published on martial arts prior to Sun's book, however, none of the books presented the theory in such a profound manner. After the book was published, the Tai Ji Quan master Chen Wei Ming (陳微明), who had taught martial arts to the Emperor Xuan Tang, visited Sun. Sun and Chen discussed the theories of martial arts. They agreed that to guide the natural Qi (氣) with the mind was just what Men Tzu spoke of when he talked of "the doctrine of the harmonization and theory of cultivation without harm." After their discussion, Chen requested to become a student of Sun Lu Tang and subsequently studied Xing Yi Quan and Ba Gua Zhang from Sun. Chen Wei Ming, who was also known as Chen Zeng Ze (陳曾則), wrote the third preface to Sun's Xing Yi Quan book.

By 1916, the martial arts were increasing in popularity among the people of Beijing. Sun joined forces with other local martial artists and opened the Beijing Sports Lecture Hall. Sun offered instruction with literal explanations and martial arts demonstrations. He instructed the sets together with explanations of the theories of the *Yi Jing* and the philosophy of Confucianism, Daoism, and Buddhism. On one occasion, Chen Bao Quan (陳寶泉), the president of the Beijing Higher Learning Teacher's College, attended one of Sun's lectures. After the lecture Chen paid Sun a visit and the two talked about the *Yi*

**Sun Lu Tang in
Tianjin, 1926**

Jing, Lao Zi, Zhuang Zi and the practice of the martial arts for strengthening the body. The two men were still talking at daybreak. When Chen spoke with others about his visit to Sun Lu Tang, he said that "Master Sun's knowledge and understanding was the highest among people in the martial arts and it was seldom seen among scholars." In this same year, 1916, the manuscript of Sun's second book, *The Study of Ba Gua Boxing*, was completed.

In the Spring of 1919, Sun's old acquaintance Xu Shi Chang persuaded him to enter government service. Between 1919 and 1924 Sun worked for the government in Beijing teaching martial arts. Because of his relationship to Xu, Sun became the martial arts instructor in the president's palace and was appointed a Lieutenant in the Army. Soon afterward he was promoted and also finished the manuscript for his third book, *The Study of Tai Ji Boxing*, in November of 1919.

During this period of time there had been a three year drought in Sun's home village and the poor people of the village had to beg for food. Sun went back to his home and said that he would lend them all money at a high interest rate. The rich people of the village refused because the interest was too high, the very poor had no choice and took the money. Sun had them all sign contracts binding them to the interest rate.

That year it rained in the village and everyone had a good crop. Sun returned and burned all of the contracts. He said that he set the interest rate high so that the poor people would work very hard and the rich people would not borrow. As he had predicted when he was a boy, he had become a famous martial artist and he had made the village people proud. In July 1921 Sun Lu Tang's Tai Ji book was published.

Sun's Tai Ji Quan

After scores of years of research with the arts of Tai Ji Quan, Xing Yi Quan, and Ba Gua Zhang, Sun Lu Tang developed the Sun style of Tai Ji Quan. Sun Jian Yun described this method as employing Ba Gua Zhang's stepping method, Xing Yi Quan's leg and waist methods, and Tai Ji Quan's body softness.

Sun became very well known for his Tai Ji Quan method and his ability to apply it. He was so well known that word of his skill had reached Japan. A famous Japanese martial artist was so determined to test Sun's skill that he convinced the Emperor of Japan to send him to China to fight Sun. In 1921, the Japanese martial artist came to visit Sun and, speaking through an interpreter, said, "I heard that you practice a Chinese martial art method which uses soft to overcome hard. Well, I am hard! How do you want to fight me? I will fight with any rules or any weapons." Sun turned to the interpreter and said, "Since he is a guest in our country, I will let him decide." The Japanese challenger said, "I am going to use hard strength to take your arm in a lock and break it. Let's see if you can use your soft

energy to overcome that!" Sun, who at 5'7" barely came to the Japanese man's shoulder, was willing to give it a try. Concerned that Sun could simply move his feet and get away from the lock, or wiggle his arm out of the lock, the challenger said, "I want you to overcome this technique without running around." Sun said, "I can accommodate you."

Sun had the spectators move all of the furniture aside and cleared a space on the floor. He said, "I will lie here on the floor, your students can hold my feet, and you can apply your technique. I'll even put my other arm behind my back." Sun laid on the floor and the Japanese martial artist took hold of his arm. The interpreter counted, "One, two, three!" At the count of three Sun quickly pulled his free arm out from behind his back and applied a point strike to

Sun Lu Tang with his wife Zhang Zhao Xien in 1932

his opponent's stomach. This point strike caused the Japanese challenger to loose his grip on Sun's other arm and Sun hopped up. The opponent was not so easily put off and followed Sun. Sun struck a few other points on his opponent's body and threw him into a bookcase. The book case fell on top of the challenger. The interpreter shouted, "You've hurt him!" Sun said, "He'll be all right. Tell him when he gets up and catches his breath we can try it again." His opponent, admitting defeat, refused to try again.

Sun Lu Tang was well known for his ability to do a tremendous amount of damage with a very light application. Once when he was pushing hands with a large, big boned student surnamed Li, the student became angry that Sun was so small yet could easily control him. He thought to himself, "He is so much smaller that I am, if I smash him, he will surely go flying." The student tried to *fa jing* (發勁 - emit force) and Sun lightly diverted the force as if nothing had happened. Frustrated that he could not hit Sun, the student left. Several hours later the student returned and Sun was sitting at his desk writing. The student was sweating heavily and could barely speak. Sun said, "When you were trying to hit me, I know what was on your mind." The student apologized and Sun said, "You have suffered internal damage." Handing the student the paper he had written on he said, "Take this prescription and go home and rest." The next day the student's entire arm was black.

Sun Lu Tang's second son was very angry with the student for trying to hit his father. Later, Sun traveled to Shanghai and took the student with him. Sun's son said, "This guy was trying to hurt you. He may try it again! Why are you treating him so well?" Sun said, "You are wrong. He knew that I could have damaged him badly. By only giving him a small taste, he knows that I used morality to overcome his violence and now he respects me."

In 1923, Sun was sad because his third son, Sun Huan Min (孫煥敏), had died in an accident in Shanghai in 1922. Xu gave Sun one month vacation and Sun traveled to Shanghai and Hong Zhou. While he was there Sun accepted over 100 students. At the end of 1923 the manuscript to Sun's fourth book, *The True Essence of Boxing*, was finished. In 1924 Sun quit his government position and went to Shanxi to supervise martial arts training. In July of that year, Sun's fourth book was published. Before January 1925, the manuscript for his fifth book, *The Study of Ba Gua Sword*, was completed. In November of 1927, the sword book was published.

In 1928 the president of the National Martial Arts Academy in Nanjing, Zhang Zhi Jiang (張之江), and the vice-president, Li Jing Lin (李景林), invited Sun Lu Tang to teach in Shanghai. Accompanied by his student Yang Shi Yuan (楊世垣), Sun took a boat to Shanghai. In 1924, Sun's student Chen Wei Ming had set up a Tai Ji study society in Shanghai so Tai Ji had become well known in the area. After Sun arrived in Shanghai he stayed at Chen's home for a short period. Later Sun traveled to Nanjing and was appointed the senior advisor of the internal arts program at the National Martial Arts Academy.

In the Autumn of 1928, the Jiang Su Provincial Martial Arts Academy was established in Zhong Jiang County. The Provincial President invited Sun Lu Tang to administer the school and Sun accepted the offer. Sun ran the school with his disciples Qi Gong Bo, Sun Zhen Chuan (孫振川), and Sun Zhen Dai (孫振岱). During this period of time

Li Yu Lin was one of Sun Lu Tang's top students

Sun traveled frequently between Nanjing, Shanghai, Su Zhou and Hang Zhou to instruct students.

In 1930 there was terrible flooding in Jiang Su and Zhe Jiang Provinces. In an effort to help raise money for the flood victims, Sun took a group of students in Shanghai to give a benefit martial arts performance. After Sun's students had demonstrated Sun himself took the platform and demonstrated Xing Yi Quan's *Za Shi Chui* (雜式捶) form. When his first punch was thrown, the audience could here the sound of the air rushing past his fist. When his foot stomped the ground it sounded like thunder. In the ending posture of the turning body, Sun's grey and white beard whipped in the wind. His performance was the highlight of the benefit.

In the Spring of 1931, Sun Lu Tang ignored an old custom and established a female martial arts course at the Zhe Jiang Martial Arts school. Sixty female students enrolled in the course. When he saw that the response was so overwhelming, Sun sent a telegram to Beijing and asked his daughter Sun Jian Yun to come and teach the class. After the Japanese invaded China in 1931, Sun quit his position at the Martial Arts Academy and returned to Beijing.

Sun Jian Yun says that her father always taught that the reason to practice martial arts was not to fight. He said that if one wants to fight they can use a gun. His advice to students was to practice in order to improve the health of the body. He stated that the goal of martial arts is to be healthy while you live and then die quickly. He said that if one is internally strong they will not become ill during their life and when the body is worn down by old age they will die with no lingering illness. Recent articles from mainland China report that Sun was known for having turned away students who were interested in fighting, telling them that if they wanted to fight they should go find a better teacher. Sun Jian Yun states that her father did not think there was

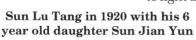

Sun Lu Tang in 1920 with his 6 year old daughter Sun Jian Yun

Some of the most famous martial artists in China meet in Shanghai, 1929. In the front row from left to right: Yang Zheng Fu (Tai Ji Quan), Sun Lu Tang (Ba Gua, Xing Yi, Tai Ji), Liu Bai Chuan (Lohan Shaolin), Li Jing Lin (Wu Dang Sword), Du Xin Wu (Natural School Boxing)

Sun Lu Tang's daughter, Sun Jian Yun, executes Xing Yi's San Ti posture at the age of 80 (1992).

any secret way to practice the martial arts. He emphasized that there were two words which describe correct practice, *Zhong He* (中和), which translates to mean "balanced" or "neutral." He recommend that students follow the principles of the style, but never practice one thing too much. The practice must be balanced. Sun Jian Yun said, "Just as when you are hot, you take off some clothing or when you are cold, you put on more clothing, when you practice you seek a balance."

Sun Jian Yun remembers when she was young watching her father practice in their home. She said that they lived in an old style home, the only thing dividing the rooms was a cloth that hung down from the ceiling. The room Sun practiced in was a bit too small for the form he performed and at one point in the form he would kick out quickly and hit the cloth which divided the rooms. She reports that her father was so exact in his forms practice that everyday he kicked the same spot. After several months he wore a hole in the cloth where he had been kicking it. Her mother would patch up the hole, however, several months later a new hole would appear in the exact same spot.

Sun's Fast Feet

Sun Lu Tang's ability to apply Ba Gua Zhang's quick footwork methods and fast stepping changes was legendary. Sun Jian Yun remembers that on one occasion Sun went to a friend's house to visit. When the friend heard the bamboo front door rattle he immediately poked his head into the room to see who it was. Sun had already crossed the room and was sitting in a chair on the other side. The friend exclaimed, "How did you get there so fast." Sun said, "That's from Ba Gua Zhang practice."

On another occasion a famous martial artist nicknamed "Nose" Li wanted to challenge Sun. All of his friends said that he was crazy because Sun was too fast. Li was persistent and Sun finally agreed. The two faced each other and before Li could get ready Sun was already behind him and had kicked him in the backside. People witnessing the fight told Li he should not have even tried against someone as fast as Sun.

In 1928 Sun went to Shanghai to teach at a big martial arts association school. When he arrived, there were 30 or 40 people who were eager to see him demonstrate his already legendary skill. Sun said, "You can all chase me, if anyone can grab my sleeve or gown, then you have *gong fu*." They all chased him around the room, but none could grab him or his clothing.

In 1931, when Sun Jian Yun was 17 years old, she learned about her father's fast footwork first hand. Sun was visiting a martial arts school in a mountainous area of China. Sun, who was then 70 years old and dragged a walking stick behind him wherever he went, asked the students to chase him up a hill. They, including Sun Jian Yun, all ran fast, but could not keep up with him. When they reached the top, he was standing in a doorway showing no signs of fatigue. He said, "You all look as if you need a rest."

Ba Gua Zhang instructor Liu Xing Han (劉興漢), now 85, of Beijing reports that when he was young and studying with his teacher Liu Bin (劉斌), Sun would often come and help him with his Ba Gua practice when Sun was

Sun Lu Tang in Shanghai, circa 1930

visiting his friend Liu Bin.   Sun and Liu Bin were classmates under Cheng Ting Hua.   Liu Xing Han remembers that every time Sun Lu Tang observed him walking the circle Sun would yell, "Faster, faster!" Sun was well known for his fast footwork and always emphasized this component of Ba Gua Zhang training when teaching students.

Sun Jian Yun reports that Sun was always very respectful of his mother.   Her grave site was ten miles away from where he lived when he was in Bao Ding.   She says that on occasion Sun would walk the ten miles to his mother's grave bowing every five steps.   He walked so fast that, even though he paused to bow every five steps, students accompanying him had a hard time keeping up.

Sun's demonstrations of skill were not limited to his ability to move quickly.   One time when he was visiting the Jiangsu Martial Arts Academy, the school officials asked him to give a demonstration. The room he was in was small and crowded with people.   There was not any room to move around so Sun went over to a wall and placed the side of one foot against the bottom of the wall (where the floor and the wall meet) and stood with his shoulder and arm flat against the wall (the arm hanging down by his side).   He then lifted the other foot off of the ground by raising his knee as high as it would go.   His foot, shoulder and arm remained pressed against the wall.   The group looked at Sun as if to say, "That wasn't very impressive."   Sun said, "Why don't a few of you try that."   Try as they might, none of them could keep their balance.   Standing in this position against a wall one who has not been trained cannot shift the weight to the leg which is next to the wall.   They asked Sun, "How could you do that?"   Sun replied that his body had no one center of balance.   His whole body was the center.

Sun's Death

According to Sun Jian Yun, her father used the *Yi Jing* (*The Book of Changes*) to predict the exact date and time of his death.   The year of his death (1933) a German doctor in a Western hospital had examined Sun and said he had the body of a 40 year old (Sun was 73).   Shortly afterward Sun said that he wanted to return to Bao Ding because he had not been there in 17 years.   When he went to Bao Ding he took on 18 new Tai Ji students and said that these were his last students. After he had taught these students what he wanted them to learn, he went back to Beijing and announced that in one month he would die. A good friend of Sun's had died recently and so his family thought that he was just depressed and would get over it.   At the time, Sun Jian Yun was taking care of her parents.   The first and third sons had already died and the second son was living in Shanghai.   Sun Lu Tang told

Sun Lu Tang's Grave Site in Wan County in Hebei Province near the city of Bao Ding

Sun Jian Yun, "We should return to Bao Ding now. I want to be buried there and it will be too much trouble to take my body back when I am dead."

Sun, his wife, and daughter went back to Wan County and Sun stopped eating. He said, "I came into this world empty and I will go out empty." He did nothing but sit in meditation most of the day and would only drink water. Sun told his daughter not to cry after he died. He left his daughter with instructions concerning what she should do when he was gone. He said he would die sitting up. They were to wait for one half hour after which they could lay his body down. After he was laying down he said his son and daughter could then weep for him.

On the day he had predicted he would die, Sun was sitting in a chair meditating. His family and friends were trying to talk to him, but he wasn't paying attention. He didn't want to put on any clothes that day because he said he wouldn't need them. On three different occasions he opened his eyes and asked what time it was. The third time he said "Good-bye," closed his eyes, and died. It was 16 December 1933. The room Sun died in was the same room he had been born in. The house was old and made of mud bricks. He was buried in his home village. One year later his wife died and was buried next to him.

There is a famous story that says that just before Sun died his students asked him what was the secret to internal martial arts training.

This story states that Sun wrote a character in his hand, showed it to his students and then died. The character he had written was the character for "practice." Sun Jian Yun, who was with her father when he died, said that this story is not true. However, she said that he did say that if there was any secret to internal arts it was simply to practice hard.

Sun Jian Yun also relates a very mysterious story concerning Sun's death. She says that three days after her father died, she returned to Beijing with her mother. Sun's body had not been buried because it was custom to have the funeral 30 to 60 days after the individual's death. The only family members left at home were Sun's second son and his wife and the wive's of Sun's eldest and third son. Sun's eldest son and third son had both already passed away (1929 and 1922 respectively). On one particular day shortly after Sun Jian Yun had left, Sun's second son, Sun Cun Zhou (孫存周), had gone to visit neighbors and his wife was the only person at home. A stranger, a young man in his thirties, came to the house and asked if this was the home of Sun Lu Tang. Sun Cun Zhou's wife said, yes this is his home, but he has recently passed away. The young man held out a thick envelope and said, "Several weeks ago I met an old white bearded man on a bridge. He gave me this envelope and asked me to come to the home of Sun Lu Tang on this day and give this envelope to his closest living relative." Sun Cun Zhou's wife took the envelope, however, she could not read so she sent for her husband. When Sun Cun Zhou arrived he looked at the young man and said, "What is this all about? We do not know you!" The young man explained about the envelope, but Sun Cun Zhou did not want to listen. He was a very stubborn man and thought that this stranger was very rude to disturb the family so soon after Sun's death. He told the young man to take the envelope and go away. The young man said, "If you do not take this envelope, you will regret it." Sun Cun Zhou refused to listen and the young man left.

Some of Sun Lu Tang disciples had gathered at the home by that time and were furious that Sun Cun Zhou did not at least look at what was in the envelope. They immediately ran after the young man, however, when they went outside he was no where to be found. Sun Jian Yun states that she does not know what might have been in the envelope, but she is sure that it was something from her father.

Sun Cun Zhou

Of Sun Lu Tang's three sons, Sun Cun Zhou was the most skilled in the martial arts. Sun's first son, Sun Xing Yi, was not interested in martial arts and did not study much. Sun Xing Yi (born around 1891) died in 1929 of illness. Sun's third son, Sun Huan Min, studied and taught his father's martial arts, however, he died in an accident in 1922, at the age of 25, in Shanghai. He was performing gymnastic exercises on a high bar and fell, breaking his ribs. The ribs punctured an internal organ and Sun Huan Min died of complications.

Sun Lu Tang in Shanghai with his second son Sun Cun Zhou

Sun Cun Zhou was a stubborn man and somewhat arrogant when he was young. In his later years he became much less arrogant and there is a story that is still told in China about the incident that humbled him. The story states that when Sun Lu Tang was living in Beijing his skill had been unbeatable and his moral integrity was high. People everywhere sought to learn from him and those who did were very proud of the fact that they were his students. Sun Cun Zhou longed for recognition of the same sort, however, lacking his father's wisdom, the impatience of youth and the proficient skills gleaned from his father's training yielded only an aggressive and ruthless boxer. As such he was always looking for another local victory in combat to build his reputation.

One day a stranger arrived in Beijing and proceeded to socialize with the well known boxers in town. As soon as Sun Cun Zhou heard about him, he immediately sought him out and challenged him to a match. As soon as the stranger agreed, Sun Cun Zhou attacked suddenly. The stranger quickly parried and simultaneously plucked out one of Sun Cun Zhou's eyes. He then lectured Sun Cun Zhou and told him, "This is your lucky day. You are fortunate we met on this day and in this way. You are fortunate to be the son of a boxer as great and renown a man as your father. And you are extremely lucky that I took only one eye and left you the other. Now go forward with your life, but change your heart for if you should by chance lose your other eye, your whole life will surely be a total loss."

The story continues by saying that several days later Sun Lu Tang sought out the stranger and thanked him for giving his son a much needed lesson of life that was too bitter a pill for his own father to

Sun Lu Tang's Five Books

administer. Although this is a great story, Sun Jian Yun says that it is not true. She says that her brother did lose an eye, but he lost it in an accident, not a fight. She also said that her brother did not fight after he lost the eye because only having one eye was a great disadvantage in a fight. Sun Cun Zhou became a humble man after loosing his eye, but it was not at the hand of another boxer.

Sun Lu Tang's Diary

In addition to the envelope mentioned above, another of Sun's important documents was also lost. Sun Jian Yun said that her father kept a dairy until he was 60 years old. He did not like to talk to people a lot, but he kept records of everything; what he had learned from his teachers, people he taught, people he fought, etc. in his diary. For Sun's 60th birthday (a very important birthday to the Chinese) several dozen of his students came to Beijing. Sun's diary was on the bookshelf in his home. After everyone left the party, the diary was gone. After Sun Lu Tang died his daughter put an ad in the paper asking whoever borrowed the book to please return it and she would make it available to all of his students. No one returned the diary, however, later she found out that one of his live-in students had taken it and had given it to his son. Later she finally tracked down the son, but it was after the Cultural Revolution and the diary had been destroyed.

Sun Lu Tang's grave site also suffered during the Cultural Revolution. In 1966, the Red Guard came to Sun's grave site to rob its contents. They figured since he was famous he must have been wealthy and had some of his valuables buried with him. All they found was a few coins and Sun's sword. They took the coins and threw the sword on the ground. Someone in the village retrieved the sword and put it in a safe place. Later the villager presented the sword to Sun Jian Yun and she subsequently donated it to the government as a national treasure. In 1982, Sun style enthusiasts helped Sun Jian Yun restore Sun Lu Tang's grave site.

Sun Jian Yun, who at 80 years old is full of life and appears very healthy, states that her father was always a humble and honest man, he was never proud or arrogant. Although the only formal schooling he received was between the ages of seven and nine, he was a respected scholar. He wrote five books during his lifetime. The first book, *The Study of Xing Yi Quan* was published in 1915, the second book, *The Study of Ba Gua Boxing* in 1916. His Tai Ji Quan book (*The Study of Tai Ji Quan*) was published in 1921, his book *The True Essence of Boxing* was published in 1924, and his Ba Gua sword book (*The Study of Ba Gua Sword*) was published in 1927. When Sun Lu Tang died he was two-thirds finished with what was to be his sixth book. This book, *The Study of Xing Yi Spear*, was never published.

Sun Jian Yun says that there was a scholar named Liu Zhun Li who was ranked number one in the last imperial examinations given in China. After Liu read a few of Sun's books he was convinced that a martial artist could not have really written them. Most martial artists of the day were illiterate and uneducated. Liu went to visit Sun and said, "You didn't write these books. Who wrote them for you?" Sun told the visitor that he had in fact written them himself. Liu, convinced that Sun was not telling the truth, grilled Sun all day on the literary classics, the *Yi Jing*, and mathematics. He was not able to stump Sun on any subject. Liu finally said, "You are a master of both the literary and martial arts."

Sun Lu Tang, who throughout his life accumulated such nicknames as "Tiger Head Hero," "First Hand Under the Sky," "and "Smarter Than An Active Monkey," is respected as a giant in the martial arts and master of his generation.

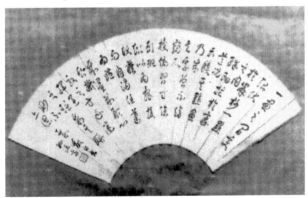

Sun Lu Tang's calligraphy painted on a fan

Sun Lu Tang's Xing Yi Quan:
An Interview with Sun Jian Yun

The following interview with Sun Jian Yun occurred on 11, 13, and 26 September 1993 at her home in Beijing, China. Special thanks to my translators Xu Yu Hong, Huang Guo Qi, and Ren Jun.

What aspect of Xing Yi Quan training did your father emphasize the most?

San Ti Shi (Trinity Posture), it is like the foundation of a building. All of the various routines of Xing Yi start from this posture. One of my father's students, Qi Gong Bo, practiced nothing but *San Ti Shi* for the first three years of his practice. Everyday he came to practice and stood in this posture without asking to be taught anything else. He eventually became my father's very best Xing Yi student.

What were some of the points your father emphasized when teaching the *San Ti* posture?

The head is held in a naturally straight position and relaxed. The neck is straight. There are three vertical lines one must pay attention to. The first is maintaining a vertical line from the heel of the forward leg to the front of the knee of the forward leg. If you drop a straight line down from the knee cap, it should be in line with the heel. There should also be a straight line from the hip to the back heel. This is the second vertical line. The third vertical is the forward index finger. It is pointing straight up and in line with the toes of the front foot.

The knees should have the feeling as though they are closing inward and the heels should feel as if they are pushing outward. The toes should feel as if they are grasping the earth. The shoulders are relaxed and the elbows sink down. The lead elbow is rotated inward so that it points straight down. The forward index finger is held at mouth level. The knuckle of the thumb on the lower hand is just below the navel. The thumb on the forward hand is flat (pointing straight out to the side). The front palm is hollow and the hand has the intention of grabbing. The front hand pushes forward and the back hand draws back. The back foot is at a 45 degree angle. The heel of the front foot is in line with the ankle bone of the back foot. The tongue is on the palate and the spine is straight. Breath through the nose and place the intention on the *dan tian*. The body is in a relaxed and natural position. Feel the strength of the whole body.

This posture has four animal characteristics: chicken's leg, dragon's body, bear shoulders and tiger's head embrace. The chicken's leg means that most of the weight is on the back leg. The dragon's body means that the body is folded into three sections. This means that the legs are bent and the hips are slightly bent creating three sections of the body. The bear shoulders means that the neck is straight and the head is held erect, the tiger's head embrace means that the arms hold strength like a tiger embracing the head of its prey. The strength of the body is held back with the intention of a tiger getting ready to pounce out of its cave and jump on its prey. This posture is the fundamental posture for everything else in Xing Yi.

What is the weight distribution between the front and back legs?

If one maintains the three verticals, the weight distribution will naturally be correct.

One thing that I must mention to you. The *San Ti* posture that appears in my father's book was changed when my father was about sixty years old. In the book, the front hand is shown with the fingers pointing straight out (see photo 1). When he was sixty he changed the front had position so that the fingers pointed upward and the wrist was bent. Because his book had already spread widely by the

San Ti Posture 1   **San Ti Posture 2**

time he changed this posture, I suggested that he take a photograph of himself in the new posture so that when I taught people the posture later and they pointed to his book to say I was wrong I could show them this picture (see photo 2).

Why did he change the posture?

He felt that when the hand was held out straight the *Qi* (氣) was projected out of the hand. He said that this was good for fighting, but was not good for cultivation. When cultivating the *Qi*, one should keep the *Qi* in the body. When the hand is held up, the *Qi* is held in the hand and recirculated.

What forms did your father's complete Xing Yi system contain?

He taught *San Ti Shi* (trinity standing), *Wu Xing Quan* (Five element fists), *Wu Xing Lian Huan* (Five Elements Linking set), *Wu Xing Sheng Ke* (Five elements creative and destructive fists), the twelve animal styles, *Za Shi Chui* (mixed form beating), *An Shen Pao* (stable body pounding) and *Ba Shi* (eight forms). Everything is in his book except for the *Ba Shi*.

So he did not teach other popular Xing Yi forms such as *Shi Er Hong Chui* or *Ba Zi Gong*?

No.

What Xing Yi weapons did he teach?

He taught the straight sword, the broadsword, and the spear. Before he died he was two-thirds finished with his sixth book which was to detail the Xing Yi spear set. Before he died he gave me the material and asked me to finish the book. However, the material was stolen from me before I had the chance to finish the book.

What was his favorite weapon?

The Ba Gua straight sword. He liked that the straight sword has blades on both sides.

Did he learn the Ba Gua sword form that he put into his book *The Study of Ba Gua Sword* from Cheng Ting Hua, or did he create that form himself?

He created that form himself based on what he had learned from Cheng Ting Hua.

What was his training sequence when teaching Xing Yi and how long did students practice one form before being taught another?

Sun Jian Yun teaches Xing Yi Quan in Japan, September 1987

It usually varied from one student to the next, however, typically a student would first spend at least one week on *San Ti Shi*, then they would be taught *pi quan* (splitting fist) and practice that for at least two weeks. Next they would spend at least one week on each of the other four elements. After that the sequence followed what is written in the book. He did not teach *Ba Shi* to many people. He taught it to me and I wrote a small book on this set. However, the book was never published.

How long did he recommend his students practice standing in *San Ti Shi* everyday?

He recommended that they work their way up to one hour. Beginning students would stand as long as they could on one leg, then change to the other leg and stand as long as they could on that leg. Then they would rest for a while and practice again. Step-by-step they would improve and eventually they could stand for one hour at a time.

In the Xing Yi book, your father starts standing in the *Wu Ji* posture, then transitions to the *Tai Ji* posture before executing the *San Ti* posture. Were each of these postures held, or was it a smooth transition from *Wu Ji* to *San Ti*?

From the *Wu Ji* (無極) posture, after the *Qi* sinks to the *Dan Tian* (丹田) and the mind is calm, one transitions smoothly from *Wu*

45

Ji to *Tai Ji* (太極) and then to the *San Ti* posture. The intermediate positions are not held static.

In some Xing Yi schools, when students practice the five elements the postures are held at each step of the form. Did your father use this method?
No. The only posture that was held stable was the *San Ti* posture. When *pi quan* was practiced, the *San Ti* posture was held at the end of each *pi quan* execution on the right and on the left. However, in the other elements, the postures were not held. The student moved smoothly and continuously through the forms. Since the forms began and ended with the *San Ti* posture, this was the only posture that was held stable.

Why did your father believe that practice of the five elements was important?
He felt that the five elements practice strengthens the physiological function of the five *Yin* organs and thus helped to harmonize one's internal Qi. If one were to overemphasize one of the elements, this harmonization would be lost. He taught that everything in the boxing is practiced in accordance with natural principles. When the body is in a harmonized natural state and the movements are natural and elegant, not tight and stiff, one can have an incredible amount of power.

My father was small and looked weak, however, he was very powerful. I witnessed several of his challenge matches where he defeated an opponent with very little movement and what appeared to be a small force.

Frequently people talk about three skill levels in the internal martial arts, namely *Ming Jing* (明勁), *An Jing* (暗勁), and *Hua Jing* (化勁). How did your father define these terms and how were these levels practiced?
Ming Jing means firm energy. The power and force is obvious. Unless a student was very old, my father started all his beginning students practicing the *ming jing* level of training. In Xing Yi practice this meant that the student's expression of force in each of the movements was obvious, such as the foot making an audible stomp on the ground when stepping. The *ming jing* training develops all of the basic skills and strengthens the bones. The *ming jing* skills had to be perfect before the student was taught to practice the *an jing* skills. The *ming jing* level of training was practiced for a relatively long period of time before the student was taught the *an*

jing skills. My father felt that if the student did not have the skills perfected at the *ming jing* level, they could never get the *an jing* level skill even if they were taught very deeply. The body had to be ready to progress. How long a student stayed at the *ming jing* level depended on how long it took them to master that level. Every student was different.

When the student was ready for the *an jing* skills, which meant that the body alignments and timing of the movements in the *ming jing* training were correct, my father would teach them to soften all their movements and make them very smooth. The feet no longer make a stomping sound and the body relaxed. The movements are the same as those in the *ming jing* level, however the student begins to learn how to refine the movements. My father felt that this level of training increased the tendon power.

Whereas the change from *ming jing* to *an jing* required the teacher to change the student's training, the progression from *an jing* to *hua jing* is natural. The practitioner reaches the *hua jing* level when the *an jing* skills become highly refined. When all of the rough edges have been ground away the *hua jing* level will develop naturally.

When your father taught the twelve animal styles, did he teach students to specialize in one or more of the animals to use in fighting?

No, there was no emphasis on one style or another. He left it to the student to decide which specialty they would like to use in fighting. My father felt that the martial arts were to be practiced for three reasons. First was to maintain one's own health, second was to defend one's self and third was to defend others. In order to gain the full health benefits one should practice all of the styles equally. Otherwise there will be imbalance. When the art is applied to fighting, naturally each student will have techniques which are best suited to them. My father left it up to the students to decide which style best suited them. He felt that it was important that they understand and develop these skills on their own.

My father also taught disciples and students in public classes differently. The students in the public classes could practice what they were interested in. My father told the disciples what they were going to practice. When my father taught Qi Gong Bo, he made him stand in *San Ti Shi* for three years. Qi never asked for anything more and so when my father would teach a class, Qi would come and stand in *San Ti Shi* while my father taught everyone else. Finally, after three years, my father approached Qi and said, "You are ready." Qi was my father's best Xing Yi student.

Sun Jian Yun at home, September 1993

My father also gauged how deeply he taught a student by how much interest they displayed. If a student practiced hard physically and also conducted intellectual research to learn the philosophy of the art, my father taught them more than other students who did not show such interest.

What happened to Qi Gong Bo?

He died from starvation in 1958. There was a bad harvest and not many people had food to eat.

How many of your father's students are still alive?

I only know of three of my father's direct student who are still alive today. Besides myself, there are two others. One is Yang Shi Yuan (楊世垣), who is now 88 years old and lives in Shanghai. He received the deep teaching from my father, however, during the Cultural Revolution his hip was shattered so he cannot practice today. The other student of my father's who is still alive is Jia Shou Qing (賈綏卿). He lives in Wan County and was one of the eighteen final students that my father accepted shortly before he died. Jia is now 87 years old.

Sun Lu Tang's Calligraphy

**The entrance to Sun Lu Tang's tomb
Wan County, Hebei Province**

Xing Yi Quan Xue

The Study of
Form-Mind Boxing

形意拳學

by Sun Lu Tang

孫祿堂　著

Translation Notes

1. The pronunciation of the Chinese characters is in accordance with the "Scheme For The Chinese Phonetic Alphabet."

2. The months and dates in prefaces and postscript are according to the Chinese lunar calendar.

3. The words, phrases, or sentences translated by the translater with a meaning different from the original version or with further explanation are explained under the topic "Footnotes" and are indicated with a superscripted numeral.*

Albert Liu
San Francisco, CA

* Footnotes which are noted with a (T) at the end of the footnote are the translator's footnotes. All other footnotes were taken from translations of Sun Jian Yun's personal footnotes to her father's book.

First Preface

It is deemed that all martial arts can trace their roots to Da Mo.[1] The martial arts have developed into many branches in which the true is often mingled with the false. Some do not look so attractive though they have been put into use. Some are rather good looking but come to failure for lack of actual effect. According to those who are adapt in martial arts, Tai Ji is the first for learning the essence of martial arts. The twelve sections of Cotton Palms in Ba Ji[2] taught in secular society is at most what an ordinary man can do. While those which are absorbed in respiration and breathing, such as Wu Qing[3] and Ba Duan Jin[4], become busy and bustling when facing an attack. Xing Yi has the same foundation as Tai Ji with its own expansion. It has no limit in outlay. Anyone, including elderly, literates, women, and girls, can practice it. Once the principle and essence are grasped by the practitioner, whoever it is, extraordinary resort will occur.

A hunchbacked old man has caught five cicada on a high tree without falling down and continues his work. A strong man at Lu Lian jumps into the torrent, sinks into the waves, and comes out of the water. A cook has killed thousands of cows through nineteen years and his knife used for this killing is still like a new one. Though there are many such fables written by Zhuang Zi[5], there are also many unusual facts in usual life which were used as the basis for him to create his stories. I have been told that Master Guo Yun Shen was strong enough to push down a wall. He asked five strong young men to hold out a long rod and push the head of the rod against his belly. All the five young men fell down on the ground after retreating five or six steps when he bulged his abdomen suddenly. However, he had never treated others badly with his unusual skill during his lifetime. As Mr. Sun Lu Tang was his disciple, his skill level need not be detailed.

Previously I read a book called *Sword And Boxing* written by Wan Yu You at Xin Chen with his pen name Wu Gong Shan Ren. I liked this book but I had no time to make a copy. Twenty years since then, the "Thirteen Sword Techniques" have been spread, but I cannot grasp the whole contents of the boxing. According to my memory, the essential spirit is among the three principal points Mind, *Qi*, and Force. The force is not coming from oneself, but has its origin from others. The principle is "borrowing." It is almighty and to go to all lengths to use this principle is utmost. Where the Mind and *Qi* arrive, there is the Force. Whether it has the same origin as what Mr. Sun Lu Tang taught, or both have the same origin but different branches, suffice to say that Mr. Sun Lu Tang has the knowledge. Supposing there are some others who were taught by Mr. Sun Lu Tang, I hope they will share the information to benefit others.

Zhao Hen at Xian Fan
May 1915

Footnotes:

1) Da Mo is the abbreviated form of the Chinese phonetic translation of the name Bodhidharma. Da Mo came from India to China in about 470 A.D. He is accredited with the writing of two books, one is called *The Tendon Changing Classic*, the other is *The Marrow Washing Classic*. (T) (Editor's Note: Present day research clearly indicates that the story of all Chinese martial arts, or even the Shaolin arts, originating from Da Mo is myth.)

2) Ba Ji is the name of a boxing style which is prevalent in Northern China. (T)

3) The full name is Wu Qing Xi. It is an exercise which imitates five animal movements to strengthen the limbs. (T)

4) Ba Duan Jin is also a kind of exercise set used to strengthen the tendons and increase *Qi* circulation. (T)

5) Zhuang Zi, about 369-286 B.C., was a philosopher during the Warring States period of ancient China. He developed the doctrine of Lao Zi and wrote a book called *Zhuang Zi*. It is also called *Nan Hua Jing*. (T)

Second Preface

The key for a human life full with the happiness of good health lies in how one takes care of oneself. In ancient times, there were methods of breathing which made it hard to avoid deviation from the proper way. That is why it is often refused by the men of noble character. Now we face a prosperous future for our country. People believe in sanitation for their health. However, we can find many people who are still weak with disease and children who are emaciated and easily become sick. The basic reason for this is the lack of knowledge of how to take care of oneself. Human life is much more precious than pretty jade. Knowing that one needs to take care of oneself but without knowing the way is similar to the present state of people talking about sanitation, but not doing anything about it.

I was taught that what is born before one's body is born is called "pre-natal," and what is born after one's body is born is called "post-natal." The pre-natal *Qi* is associated with the kidneys, and the post-natal *Qi* with the spleen. The pre-natal *Qi* is the essence of *Qi*. It is peaceful and keeps the spirit in calmness. The post-natal *Qi* is manifest in the practice of *Qi*. It is cultivated in moving and can excite the spirit. Water, wood, fire, earth, and metal are the five *Qi* existing respectively in the five viscera and circulating reciprocally to produce each other. Coordinating with the *Wu Xing*[1] of *Yin* and *Yang* spreading over the heaven and earth, the five *Qi* in one's body arrive at the five sensual organs and causes the spirit to produce wisdom. At the same time, when it arrives at the tendons, bones, and channels, it causes the essence to emit power. This principle can only be understood by those who have really taken care of themselves and become solid and strong, sensitive and flexible.

The book *Su Wen* indicated, "In ancient times, some understood the principle and performed in accordance with Ying and Yang." "In current times, people wallow in sensual pleasures without limit in their life; so it is easy to decay at fifty." "The *Ren*[2] channel becomes void and obstructs the earth path for a woman at her forty-ninth year. This will cause her to become withered and sterile." Hence we know that the human body can't be compared with metal or stone. Anyone who doesn't take good care of themselves will receive a premature end. My friend Mr. Sun Lu Tang sent me the book *The Study of Xing-Yi Boxing* and told me, "You can get the essence of this boxing through a profound study and receive immeasurable benefits through diligent training." After a period of practice, I asked him for advice again. He said, "The five elements boxing comes from *Wu Ji*[3]. What is called Wu Ji is pre-natal and is an extreme subject of the human being. It is without idea and body. It's the origin of harmony, and the primary source of *Tai Ji*[4], *Yin-Yang*, and *Dong Jing*. Everything is born in a state of the back being to *Yin* and the front facing *Yang*. Everything is a *Tai Ji*. From *Wu Ji* shifts out *Tai Ji*. Where the primordial *Qi* of human being comes from, the spirit of human being derives from. It is also the source of *Wu Xing* boxing, which keeps a relation with the former and thus makes change. It is this changing power that keeps the spirit calm and makes a balance between *Yin* and *Yang* in the human body. Thus it invigorates channels, promotes blood circulation, and elongates the life-span so one can enjoy longevity. This is the way to promote oneself and change from a post-natal back to a pre-natal state and realize good health. It is ignorant to take this as hearsay. It is suitable not only for young men, but for seniors, ladies and children. It has a hundred advantages without one disadvantage. It can be used to raise the health level of our race. This instruction makes me have a deep understanding not only in this set, but also in the farsighted purpose designed by Mr. Sun Lu Tang of raising the health level of the people and strengthening our country.

This Xing Yi boxing has its origin in *Wu Ji* and can coordinate with *Yin* and *Yang* and the four seasons. It can't be compared with the ancient respiration and breathing or with the current common training skills. Mr. Sun Lu Tang learned this boxing directly from master Li Kui Yuan. It is derived from the so-called *Yue Jia* boxing invented by General Yue Wu Mu[5] in the Song Dynasty. Its far origin may be traced back to the ancient originator Da Mo. It is the key of rejuvenation and the way to longevity. It has both the merits of martial arts and refined theoretical principle. I am obliged to write a preface for this book. I make strenuous efforts to do my best. However, I dare not say it is suited to the profound meaning of the book.

Ai Yu Kuan
Hou Xian of Da Xing

Footnotes:

1) *Wu Xing* indicates the fundamental five elements, i.e. wood, fire, earth, metal, and water. According to the Wu Xing doctrine, there is mutual promotion and destruction between the five elements. (T)

2) The *Ren* Channel is one of the eight special channels. Its route is from the central point between the anus and the genitals through the central line of the abdomen and chest across the throat to the root of the tongue. (T)

3) *Wu Ji* is a philosophical term. It originally means the most primary phenomenon of the cosmos. Here it means that before practicing the boxing, one should be empty in the mind, i.e. without any thought or intention. Nothing is held in the heart, there are no motives in the mind, no visual power in the eyes, no dance in the hands or feet, no movements in the body, no distinguishing between *Yin* and *Yang*, no distinction between clear and turbid. (T)

4) *Tai Ji* means that the inside of *Wu Ji* there springs forth a harmonization of the empty and the extreme (*Yin* and *Yang*). In the body, when the *Qi* is hidden inside it is the morality and when it is shown externally it is *Dao*. The circulation of *Qi* in the interior and exterior corresponds with heaven and earth and generates *Yin* and *Yang*. The internal energy of the boxing skill is the basis of the human body, therefore it is termed *Tai Ji*.

5) Yue Wu Mu was Yue Fei's title. It is said that he created Xing Yi boxing based on the classics written by Da Mo.

Third Preface

After about four years of learning Xing Yi boxing from Mr. Sun Lu Tang, I then understood that Xing Yi boxing is simple in style but profound in meaning, easy to learn but difficult to train.

Light comes from the movement of the sun and the moon. Seasons come from the alternation of heat and cold. According to the principle of *Yin-Yang* and bending-extending in nature, Xing Yi boxing has moving forward and backward, going along with and going against. Within bending-extending, the *Qi* is full without directing, the force is limitless without enforcing. This achievement is in accordance with *Yin-Yang*, along with the principle of nature, and has the same state of substance as Tai Ji. Therefore, the state of substance of Tai Ji is referred to at the beginning of this book. This point is the essence of martial arts. Lack of this knowledge will lead to the misunderstanding that Xing Yi is not Tai Ji. The state of being completely rounded-out without any break is in accordance with the principle of Tai Ji. Styles and methods are but its outer forms. There are many Tai Ji boxers who perform the Long Style[1] and the Thirteen Postures[2] without understanding the state of being completely rounded-out without any break. They are really not the true Tai Ji boxers. Mr. Sun Lu Tang is versed in Xing Yi, Bua Gua, and Tai Ji and thus can merge them together. It will benefit the body and mind deeply for martial artists to make a modest study on this principle.

Chen Zeng Ze
Qi Shui
March 1919

Footnotes:

1) Here Long Style means the long style of the Tai Ji Boxing. (T)

2) Thirteen Styles is an abbreviation of the name "Tai Ji Thirteen Styles." In the Tai Ji boxing, the movement of the hands has eight directions, while the feet has five step positions. The eight directions are four proper square directions plus four angle directions. The five step positions are forward, backward, leftward, rightward and the center. The eight directions represent the Ba Gua; the five step positions represent the five elements. (T)

Author's Preface

As we know, heaven and earth were first, then came humankind. People work and create other things. This is the natural tendency. The way of becoming prosperous and strong lies in the bracing up of the people. The important point is to brace up the spirit. A strong country cannot be composed of weak people. We cannot make people strong without physical training. To brace up the people through physical training is the way to strengthen the country. There was prejudice in the old days. Literates despised martial arts as martial artists were short of literary learning. Now the country will be improved through reforming affairs. Martial arts has been put into the curriculum in schools so that students can be cherished on both literary and military sites. This is a good way.

I have been unceasing in my literary study and interest in martial arts since my childhood. I don't want to be bold with powerful force, but hope to have the proper way to health. The real courage is not based on bold force, but on the interrelationship of hardness and softness without boldness. There is a common saying that the principle of martial arts training is the same as that of literary learning. Both have the same value and importance. Literates do not like martial arts seeing that common martial arts are too bold and lack elegance.

As for Xing Yi boxing, it includes Tai Ji, Wu Xing, and Ba Gua. According to their origin, both Tai Ji and Ba Gua branches, as well as external and internal schools, have the same source. That different branches and groups derived and developed from the same origin is a historical tendency. I have learned martial arts for more than forty years and will comment on what I heard from my master and read from the old boxing manuals. I will just try to explain it and dare not make any arbitrary inference.

I heard from my master that Xing Yi boxing was invented by the ancient originator Da Mo and was called *Nei Jing*. It was developed by Yue Wu Mu[1] in the Song dynasty. During the Yuan and Ming dynasties no related books could be found and it was almost not handed down. At the end of Ming and the beginning of Qing dynasty, at Zhu Feng[2] in the east suburb of Pu county, there was a person called Ji Ji Ke who was also known as Ji Long Feng. He was

60

excellent in martial arts and full of experience. It is he who got several volumes of the martial arts manual of Yue Wu Mu at Zhong Nan mountain and acquired its essence. He imparted it to Mr. Cao Ji Wu[3], who was the winner of the military examination in 1693 Kang Xi period of the Qing dynasty and performed the duty of brigade general at Jing Yuan in Shanxi Province. During his term of office, he had no other hobby but to teach martial arts to entertain himself. He imparted his *gong fu* to Mr. Dai Long Bang[4] of Shanxi origin. Mr. Dai Long Bang imparted his *gong fu* to Mr. Li Luo Neng[5] of Hebei origin. Mr. Li Luo Neng imparted his *gong fu* to Guo Yun Shen[6] of Hebei origin, Liu Qi Lan of Hebei origin, Song Shi Rong of Hebei origin, Che Yi Zhai of Shanxi origin, and Bai Xi Yuan of Jiangsu origin. They in turn imparted their *gong fu* respectively to their own students.

Mr. Guo Yun Sheng imparted his art to Li Kui Yuan and Xu Zhan Ao. Mr. Liu Qi Lan imparted to Li Cun Yi, Geng Ji Shan, and Zhou Ming Tai. I took Li Kui Yuan as my master and learned from him for several years. I once had a chance to see Yue Wu Mu's boxing manual at Mr. Bai Xi Yuan's place in Beijing. This manual was a copy and was not very detailed. There was not any explanation in it except some lines of former words that enlighten me and caused me to make up my mind to write a full explanation of the manual. I studied it carefully and imitated each posture one after another. Here I have made my best endeavor, with my limited knowledge, to write a book according to the principle and practice of the original one.[7] For shortcomings in this book, I earnestly look forward to obtain instruction and correction.

> Sun Fu Quan
> Wan county of Bao Ding prefecture
> January 15, 1915

Footnotes:

1) Yue Wu Mu was Yue Fei's title. It is said that he created Xing Yi boxing based on the classics written by Da Mo. (T)

2) Zhu Feng is in the area east of Pu County in Shanxi Province. The present name of this place is Zhang Ying Zhen Village, Yung Ji County, Shanxi Province.

3) Cao Ji Wu won first place in the martial arts examinations three times during the reign of the Kang Xi Emperor. He was later appointed governor of the Jing Yuan in Shanxi.

4) Dai Long Bang was a native of Tai Gu County in Shanxi.

5) Li Luo Neng, who was also known as Li Fei Yu and Li Neng Ran, was a native of Shen County in Hebei Province. He lived from 1806 through 1890. Although he is usually listed as a student of Dai Long Bang, some say that he actually received his instruction from Dai's son, Dai Wen Xun.

6) Guo Yun Shen was from Hebei Province, Shen County, Ma Village. For more information on Guo, see the section of this book on Sun Lu Tang's biography.

7) Sun Lu Tang saw a copy of the boxing manual which was attributed to Yue Fei at the home of Bai Xi Yuan. He read the manual and memorized it. He studied the postures in the book and used this knowledge to write his own Xing Yi manual.

Directions To The Reader

1. This book is divided into Part I and Part II. The main points are selected and brought forward. At the beginning of the Part I, the study on the Wu Xing caused by the seperation of the heaven and earth is explained. Accompanied with it is the postures with their explanation. These points are the foundation of Xing Yi boxing. The items in the Part I include the first part that covers five sections on general principles, narrating from Xing Yi Wu Ji to the important points of practice. The second part covers seven chapters narrating from splitting fist to the reciprocal "creation and destruction" of the Wu Xing. The set should be practiced according to this sequence.

That everything is derived from the heaven and earth of Xing Yi is the principle narrated in Part II. The items in the Part II narrate from the first chapter on dragon style to the fourteenth chapter on *An Shen Pao*. In these items there are single and double play. The former is performed by oneself and the later is performed by a pair of opponents in competition. The pair may be differentiated from each other as A and B or upper and lower hands. Every change of opening and beginning, advancing and retreating, stretching and contracting, is explained in detail. Every motion and rest should be performed according to the rule. Through training in this way, the general functions of the set may be obtained. It is a great achievement out of nothing.

2. This book is for practice. The focal point is on the practical benifits. The manner of writing is easy to understand without flowery words. So it does not stick to rhetorics.

3. In this book all citations coincide with the basic principle. It's entirely different from those books full with deliberate exaggerations. It should be strictly separated from what is called heresy.

4. The property of the practice sets has as their aim to maintain the proper *Qi*. It can't be compared with such books as *Eight Section Training* and others written about methods of punching and kicking. The way to practice the twelve styles of boxing (twelve animals) are compiled in a continuous integrity so that it is clear at a glance.

5. There are many kinds of physical training, among them only Xing Yi boxing is based on the natural principle of heaven and earth and makes use of pure and proper *Qi*. Everyone, men and women, young and old, can learn and practice it. There is no need to bend the waist and legs too much, nor to jump high. It can be practised in common dress. So it is rather elegant in the world of martial arts training.

6. In other kinds of martial arts some are hard, some are rather soft, and some emphasize circulating *Qi*. They do not have the wonderful effects as this set has. It is really out of the conventional patterns.

7. This set of twelve styles (twelve animals) is a training of the integral body including both physical and spiritual sites. Through this training, normal people can improve and strengthen their own health, patients embarassed with chronic disease and unable to move freely can recover.

8. There is a picture for each style of the set. Each form is composed of different postures, and all forms are organized into an integral unit. The principle and its property can be easily understood so as to correctly develop its wonderful effects.

9. All pictures are presented for accuracy. Wonderful effects may be obtained through serious immitation and dilligent training.

Part One

The Study of Xing Yi in Wu Xing Since the Separation of Heaven and Earth

形意混沌闢開
天地五行學

General Principle

The Study of Wu Ji in Xing Yi

Before training, there is no thought or intention, no figure or image, no self or others, only *Qi* exists in the chaos of the body. The state is called *Wu Ji*[1] in Xing Yi. Without knowing the principle of "inverse motion," people always rigidly adhere to the principle of the "direct motion nature[2]." Hence the internal *Qi* is restrained and things cannot be properly realized due to an obscure mind that causes the body to be weak. They do not know the principle of health that extreme *Yang* leads to *Yin* and extreme *Yin* leads to death. However, sages can be versed in the way of inverse motion, can control the relation between *Yin* and *Yang*, manage the principle of creation, direct *Liang Yi*[3], grasp the key points, and go back to the pre-natal from the post-natal realm to settle at the original position whence the body becomes an integral unit[4]. Its way is nothing more than the principle of stretching and contracting as in post-natal Wu Xing and Ba Gua boxing[5]. This is called the generation of *Qi* from *Wu Ji*[6].

The beginning point is *Wu Ji*. The posture of which is facing to the proper direction, hanging down both hands, and keeping a 90 degree angle between the two feet. This means going along with the natural principle.

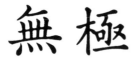

Wu Ji

Footnotes:

1) *Wu Ji* is a philosophical term. It originally means the most primary phenomenon of the cosmos. Here it means that before practicing the boxing, one should be empty in the mind, i.e. without any thought or intention. Nothing is held in the heart, there are no motives in the mind, no visual power in the eyes, no dance in the hands or feet, no movements in the body, no distinguishing between *Yin* and *Yang*, no distinction between clear and turbid. Have the mind and consciousness in a calm state. That is the situation of no intention. (T)

2) The "principle of inverse motion" means that the post-heaven returns to the pre-heaven when the internal energy and external nature are cultivated. When humans involve themselves in material attractions, Yin and Yang become disharmonious and the body constitution becomes weak, this is "direct motion nature."

3) *Liang Yi* is the separation of *Yin* and *Yang* which evolves from *Tai Ji*. *Liang Yi* is represented symbolically by a solid line which corresponds to *Yang* and a broken line which corresponds to *Yin*. It represents the one becoming two. The one *Qi* of *Tai Ji* becomes two separate forces. It is also called the two great powers. *Liang Yi* is related to the heaven and earth. See the illustration on page 80.

4) This means that practitioners whose skills become perfectly proficient can master *Yin* and *Yang* and are able to correct the physiological functions of the internal organs in order to guide the harmonious *Qi* and return to pre-heaven, or the initial origin.

5) This refers to the expansion and contraction of the one *Qi* in Wu Xing Quan and Ba Gua Quan.

6) *Wu Ji* creates *Tai Ji*, *Tai Ji* is the one *Qi*. One *Qi* generates *Yin* and *Yang* and *Yin* and *Yang* can change in infinite ways.

Section One

The Study of Qi in the Emptiness of Xing Yi

The so-called "emptiness" can be shown by the symbol of a round circle. The so-called "existing Qi" can be shown by the symbol of a round circle with a vertical line in it[1]. The one Qi generated from the emptiness is the only real pre-natal Qi coming through inverse motion[2]. This Qi is vital as it contains a lease on life which is the root of life, the source of creation, and the basis of living and death[3]. It is the foundation of Xing Yi boxing. At the time just before the beginning of motion, the whole body is empty, but full with this Qi. There exists the foundation but it is hidden. This is the one Qi of *Tai Ji*[4].

Emptiness

Existing Qi

To begin, make a half turn to the right. Both hands hang down vertically. The left foot steps forward closing to the shin bone of the right foot. The feet form an angle of 45 degrees. The upper surface of the tongue is in contact with the upper palate, and the anus is gently lifting up. This posture is for controlling the relationship between *Yin* and *Yang*, grasping the principle of creation, directing the *Liang Yi*, managing the key points, and inversely moving the pre-natal real *Yang Qi* to avoid the post-natal false *Yang*.

The Qi of Emptiness

Footnotes:

1) The round circle symbolizes the *Wu Ji* and the circle with the vertical line symbolizes *Tai Ji*.

2) The "one *Qi* generated from emptiness" means to return to the origin and use the *Qi* of pre-heaven.

3) This *Qi* is not tranquil, it is active and changing. It contains the creative *Qi*.

4) Before the body moves, the intention of motion is generated already. Although no trace of this *Qi* is yet shown, the intention of motion already exists in the interior. This is the one *Qi* of *Tai Ji*.

5) This is the *Tai Ji* posture transformed from the *Wu Ji* posture. *Wu Ji* means voidness in the heart. *Tai Ji* means *Yin* and *Yang* start to appear in the abdomen (originally there is one, relatively there is two, two means *Yin* and *Yang*). When there is *Yin* and *Yang*, it is possible to generate all things. This fixed posture means that a situation of tranquility is generated and motion is about to begin, but motion has yet to occur. Therefore this posture seeks to master the ability to change *Yin* and *Yang* and requests that the body take charge and prepare to change the *Qi* circulation. Utilize the pre-heaven true *Yang Qi*, not the awkward *Yang Qi* of post-heaven.

Section Two

The Study of Tai Ji in Xing Yi

Tai Ji relates to earth. It relates to the spleen in the human body and to the "crossing fist" of Xing Yi boxing, in which are included four other conducts, i.e. splitting, drilling, smashing, and pounding. *Xing* means "form" and *Yi* means "mind." Being the spirit of everything, a human being can influence and reflect everything[1]. Being inside, the mind acts on everything around it, and objects, being outside, have their principle in the mind. Mind acts inside and every object forms outside[2]. Both of these sides are connected by the *Qi*.

At the beginning, the body status transitions from rest to moving. Any inclining forward or backward, toward the left side or right side is prohibited. Each part is in harmony with the other parts. The body is vertically straight. The left foot is in front of the right foot. The left heel closes to the right shin bone. The two feet form an angle of 45 degrees between them, as shown in the photograph. Relax and allow the shoulders to hang. Both elbows are close to the flanks. The two hands are held up in front of the heart, left hand below the right. The left forefinger and right middle finger stretch forward horizontally, the later is on the former, and both fingers

Tai Ji

coincide with each other. The top of the head presses up. The neck should be vertically straight. The waist settles down. Both hip bones roll inside and draw strength in balance. Both heels twist strength outside. The two legs bend slowly down, as in the photograph. The bending of the legs should be rounded out and never form a dead angle. The body should be maintained vertically straight without a slight inclination. The mind should hold no anger.

At the beginning, the mind is like a rod standing on plain ground. When the rod has been put vertically straight and stable, the mind is naturally going to calm and settle down without any inclination. At this time, the heart coincides with the mind, the mind coincides with the *Qi*, and the *Qi* coincides with the force. This is called the "Three Internal Harmonies." If the Three Harmonies do not coincide, any small deviation at the beginning will lead to a distance of a thousand miles from the principle. Special attention should be focused on this point.

This posture presents the form of cock's leg, dragon's body, bear's shoulders, and tiger's head embrace. This is what is called "one *Qi*" and includes *Si Xiang*. *The Book of Changes* says that *Si Xiang* does not part from the *Liang Yi*, and the *Liang Yi* does not part from the "one *Qi*." The one *Qi* generates substance from emptiness, whereas *Liang Yi* has its root in the one *Qi*.

The so-called "cock's leg" means independent standing posture, the "dragon body" means three-fold body posture, the "bear shoulders" means vertically straight neck of strength, the "tiger head embrace" means that the posture of the hands is like a tiger departing its cave.

Footnotes:

1) This means that it is possible to sense and understand the theory of all matter.

2) If a human can express his sincerity to deal with all matter from the bottom of the heart, all matter can be modified to expose the quality of its appearance externally. This means that the internal mind and external appearance are related to the circulation of *Qi*.

3) The *Si Xiang* (four figures) are formed by combining the *Liang Yi*. They are given names of Greater *Yang*, Lesser *Yin*, Lesser *Yang*, and Greater *Yin*. The *Si Xiang* are typically related to the four seasons: spring, summer, autumn, and winter; and the four directions: east, west, south, and north. See the illustration on page 80. (T)

Section Three

The Study of Liang Yi in Xing Yi

The so-called *Liang Yi* is the principle of moving and rest, up and down, stretching and contracting, and advancing and retreating in the boxing. The body has four branches and hundreds of bones. Stretching is *Yang* and contracting is *Yin*. Both hands embrace each other and go up towards the head. The left hand advances first, the two hands separate from each other slowly. The left hand pushes forward while the right hand draws back. Both hands move as if tearing cotton. The left hand stretches out straight, with the highest point being even with the level of the mouth. The thumb is at the level of the heart. The arm seems straight, but it is not. It seems to be bent, but it is not. The section of the arm from wrist to elbow should be in a horizontal position[1]. The right hand draws towards the heart and the inner pit of the thumb root is under the heart. The left foot steps up and then is placed down in coordination with the movement of the left hand. The rear foot remains stationary. The five fingers of both hands spread out without any contact with one another. The left thumb should be in a horizontal crossing position. The left forefinger stretches

Liang Yi

upward. The thumb and forefinger of both hands form a "tiger mouth" or semi-circle. The eye sight falls between the thumb root and forefinger tip of the left hand. Both shoulders relax and draw strength. Both hips roll in and draw strength. This is called the harmony of the shoulders with the hips. Both elbows drop down with strength which doesn't manifests itself. The rear elbow bends inside, but should never be held at a dead angle. This bending has to be rounded out as a half moon. Both knees bend inside with strength which does not manifest itself. This is called the harmony of the elbows with the knees. Both heels twist outside with strength which does not manifest itself. This is called the harmony of the hands and feet. All these three together are called the "Three Outer Harmonies."

The shoulders urge the elbows. The elbows urge the hands. The waist urges the hips. The hips urge the knees. The knees urge the feet. Always keep a vertically straight body without any inclination and maintain stable internal *Qi*. Pay attention to *Yin* while looking at *Yang*, and pay attention to *Yang* while looking at *Yin*. *Yin* coincides with *Yang*, the upper part connects with the lower part, the inside is the same as the outside. All these together form the six harmonies. The six harmonies are really the harmony of the inside with the outside. The harmony of the inside with the outside is really the harmony of *Yin* and *Yang*. The harmony of *Yin* and *Yang* gives birth to the trinity (*San Ti*).

Footnotes:

1) Editor's Note: Sun Lu Tang modified this posture around 1921 from the posture which appeared in the original book to the posture which is shown in the photograph. In the original book, the forward hand was held such that the fingertips pointed forward and the wrist was straight. Here the wrist is bent so that the fingers point up and the palm pushes forward. (See page 43.)

Section Four

The Study of Trinity in Xing Yi

The so-called Trinity (*San Ti*) denotes the three phases all together, i.e. heaven, earth, and the human being. It corresponds to the head, hands, and feet in boxing. These three phases are again divided into three sections.

The waist is the root section, on the outside is the waist, on the inside is the *Dan Tian*[1]. The back is the middle section, on the outside is the back, on this inside is the heart. The head is the top section, on the outside is the head, on the inside is the *Ni Wan*[2].

Next, the shoulder is the root section, the elbow the middle section and the hand is the top section. Lastly, the hip is the root section, the knee is the middle section, and the foot is the top section.

The principle that these three sections have three sub-sections coincides with the nine numbers of the *Luo Shu*[3]. The *Dan Shu* says that *Dao* generates *Qi* from emptiness[4]. This *Qi* generates *Yin* and *Yang*. *Yin* and *Yang* become trinity. Trinity creates everything. The so-called "*Qi* in emptiness" is the root of heaven and earth, the source of *Yin* and *Yang*, and the origin of everything. This is also called *Jing Dan*[5].

Trinity (*San Ti*)

It corresponds with the internal strength in Xing Yi boxing.

People always think about the concrete body and related phases and that internal strength often is deemed as an endeavor of the mind, or arousing *Qi* in the abdomen, etc.; so they do not know what is the internal strength in Xing Yi boxing. All these are superficial and false understanding. That is why there are so many martial artists but so rarely are there real successful ones. During study, any way of training is out of this trinity. This is the entrance of real learning and the general key in Xing Yi boxing.

Footnotes:

1) *Dan Tian* is the name of an area under the navel including the points *Guan Yuan, Shi Men, Qi Hai,* and *Ying Jiao.* Generally its center is at about two inches below the navel. (T)

2) *Ni Wan* refers to an area inside of the head which includes the "third eye" and connects with the *Bai Hui* acupuncture point at the crown of the head. (T)

3) The *Luo Shu* (Luo Book or Luo Scroll) is said to have been the origin of the *Yi Jing.* There were descriptions in a volume of the *Yi Jing* that said that the River Map came out of the Lou River and the scroll comes from Lou. Confucious believed that the River Map was the origin of the Ba Gua and the Luo Scroll was the origin of the Nine Palaces. (See illustrations on the next page.)

4) This idea comes from the *True Understanding* by Zhang Bo Duan in the Northern Song Dynasty. This is the main classic of the Daoist skill for life preservation. There is a similar meaning expressed in Chapter 42 of *Lao Zi* saying the Dao produces one, one produces two, two produces three, three produces the ten thousand things. Therefore, it is called the quotation of *Dan Shu.* Daoism refers to the universe defined as one. That one produces two means *Yin* and *Yang*, that is the heaven and earth. That two produces three means that the *Qi* of *Yin* and *Yang* produce the "gushing" *Qi.* The gushing *Qi* means the combined *Qi* of *Yin* and *Yang*, hence it is possible to produce the ten thousand things. In the boxing skill this means that *Wu Ji* produces one *Qi* and one *Qi* produces *Yin* and *Yang.* The changes of *Yin* and *Yang* in the boxing skill produce the theory of the boxing skill, namely, extending and contracting, going up and down, side-to-side and to and fro in order to initiate the infinite changes of *Yin* and *Yang*.

5) *Jing Dan* means "golden pill" in Daoism. Here it refers to the internal energy in the boxing skill.

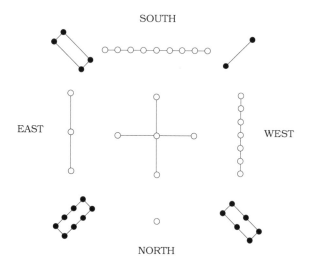

The Luo Scroll

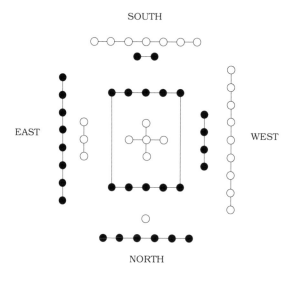

The River Map

Section Five

The Important Points of Xing Yi Practice

The important points of Xing Yi practice are as follows. The first is setting down the waist; the second is dropping the shoulders; the third is hollowing the chest; the fourth is propping up; the fifth is lifting up; the sixth is making clear crossing and following; the seventh is distinguishing the components of rising, drilling, falling, and overturning from one another.

Setting down the waist means lifting up the coccyx to raise the *Qi* of *Yang*; this belongs to the principle of the *Du*[1] channel. Dropping the shoulders means to draw back strength with the two shoulders. Hollowing the chest means to open the chest for circulating the *Qi* and allowing the *Qi* of *Yin* to go down; this belongs to the principle of the *Ren* channel. Propping up means to prop up the head, the tongue, and the hands. Lifting up means to lift up the anus. Crossing means beginning; following means falling; rising means drilling; falling means turning over. Beginning is crossing and falling is following. Rising is the beginning of crossing and drilling is the end of crossing. Falling is the beginning of following and turning over is the end of following.

The head is drilling when it is propping up and it is turning over when it is contracting. The hand is drilling when it is beginning and it is turning over when it is falling. The foot is drilling when it is rising and turning over is falling. The waist is drilling when it is beginning and it is turning over when it is falling. The crossing is concealed when beginning and crossing; the following is concealed when falling and following. Rising is going and falling is biting; but really both rising and falling are biting. To bite in rising and falling is just like the turning of waves. However, as the rising, drilling, falling, and over turning change to and fro, the elbow should always be close to the heart. All stated above are the important points of Xing Yi boxing. Understanding these important points means to find out the proper entrance of Xing Yi boxing.

Footnotes:

1) The *Du* Channel is one of the eight special channels. Its route is from the central point between the anus and the genitals through the central line of the back and across that of the head to the upper teeth. (T)

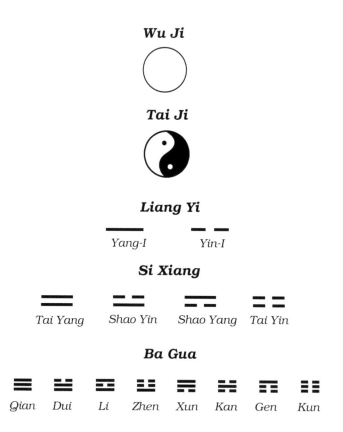

Wu Ji

Tai Ji

Liang Yi

Yang-I   Yin-I

Si Xiang

Tai Yang   Shao Yin   Shao Yang   Tai Yin

Ba Gua

Qian   Dui   Li   Zhen   Xun   Kan   Gen   Kun

The Study of
the Five Fists
of Xing Yi Quan

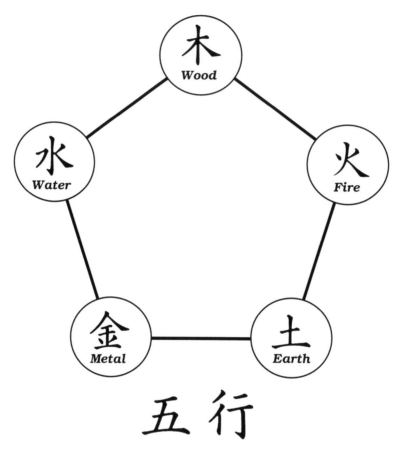

**The Five Elements
(Wu Xing)**

Chapter One

The Study of Splitting Fist (Pi Quan)

劈

拳

General Principle

The Study of Splitting Fist

The splitting fist, belonging to metal, is the beginning of the falling of *Qi*. The former four sections explain that the trinity (*san ti*) comes into being and creates everything. The trinity is always the coincidence of *Yin* and *Yang*. The coincidence of *Yin* and *Yang* is always the one *Qi* combined with that of the upper and lower and the inner and outer. So its form looks like *Tai Ji*. The *Qi* in rest forms the trinity. The *Qi* in circulation creates things. This motion is called "crossing," which belongs to earth. Earth gives birth to everything. So there are four components in crossing. According to the circulation of Wu Xing, earth produces metal. So the beginning and falling of it belongs to metal in Wu Xing and its shape is like an ax. It belongs to the lungs in the human body and forms the splitting action in the boxing. If the splitting acts with the following strength, there is mild *Qi* in the lungs. If it acts with an erroneous strength, there is perverse *Qi* in the lungs. The human body is led by *Qi*. Mild *Qi* makes the body strong, while erroneous *Qi* makes the body weak. A weak body incurs disease and its boxing will be obstructed and ineffective. Therefore, splitting fist should be studied first.

Section One

The Beginning Form of Splitting Fist

At the beginning, the left hand is falls down directly to the area of the *Qi Hai* (sea of *Qi*), then drills upward from the navel to the mouth. The hand is as if it is supporting the chin and changes into drilling forward simultaneously with the step forward of the left foot. While drilling forward, the hand is in a fist with the fist heart upward[1]. The hand is on line with the foot at the level between the eye and the mouth as its upper and lower limit. When the left foot makes a pad step forward, its distance depends on the height of the body. Normally the easiest, most comfortable stepping distance is the best. The tip of the left foot turns outward 90 degrees when it is falling down, as shown in the photograph. At this time, the crotch should be opening internally, the right hand moves from the right side close to the right flank and changes into a fist with its heart upward.

Splitting Fist - Beginning Form

Footnote:

1) Editor's Note: Throughout this book the "heart of the fist" is the palm.

2) *Qi Hai* is a spot on the channel *Ren*. It is at about one and half inches down from the navel. (T)

Section Two

The Changing Palm of Splitting Fist

When the right hand stretches out again, the right foot steps forward at the same time. The right hand turns over as it stretches out. When it arrives at the front hand, the heart (palm) of the right hand faces downward. The middle finger of the right hand is on the root of the forefinger of the left hand. Then both hands separate slowly from each other, the left hand draws back while the right hand pushes forward. The hand and foot fall into place at the same time. This is the same posture as the trinity (*San Ti*) form. All motions of both sides in this form look like the Chinese "scholar tree insect" in walking, and like bearing a shoulder pole in lifting. The number of repetitions executed before turning back depends on the space. It is not necessary to stick to the same length. However, turning back should take place after stretching out the left hand and foot. This is according to the principle that heaven is rotating toward the left. Take the left turn because splitting fist belongs to metal.

Splitting Fist - Changing Palm

Section Three

The Turning Back of Splitting Fist

When turning back, the left hand and foot turn back at the same time, the left foot is at the back as shown in the photograph. The left hand is drawn back to the left flank near the heart. The right hand and foot turn back with the body. The motion of the right hand and foot is the same as in the trinity (*San Ti*) form. Drilling, overturning, rising, falling, and advancing of the left hand and foot are the same as before. The number of repetitions depends on oneself. If there are many practitioners training together, the number of repetitions depends on the word of command made by the instructor.

Splitting Fist - Turning Back

Section Four

The Closing Form of Splitting Fist

When closing, the practitioner should come back to the original beginning place and the motions turn back to the trinity (*San Ti*). However, the right foot should make a following step, but should not be too close to the forefoot. The mind should be calmed, lift the top of the head and close the mouth. Now a short rest may be taken, but lifting the top of the head and respiration should be kept as before. The old masters pointed out that the eyes should not be looking down, but looking slightly up. The eyes looking up belongs to *Yang* and looking down belongs to *Yin*. While the eyes are looking down, the fire of *Yin* leaps up and may cause the eyes to become red and the practitioner may experience dizziness. The eyes looking up can relieve the fire of *Yin* and the head and eyes will be clear. The old masters also said that the tongue should be in contact with the upper palate. The saliva in the mouth must be swallowed down to avoid a dry mouth. These principles are the same hereafter.

Splitting Fist - Closing Form

Chapter Two

The Study of Smashing Fist (Beng Quan)

崩
拳

General Principle

The Study of Smashing Fist

The smashing fist[1], belonging to wood, is according to the principle of stretching and contracting of *Qi* and both hands going to and fro. The motion is like succeeding arrows. In the body, it belongs to the liver. In boxing, it is smashing. This is why we say that the smashing fist is like the arrow and belongs to wood. A correct smashing fist makes the *Qi* of the liver smooth, while an incorrect smashing fist will hurt the *Qi* of the liver and this will cause the spleen and stomach discord. The unsmooth *Qi* of the liver will further cause the crossing fist to lose its harmony. This fist can make the *Qi* of the liver even and in smooth running, enhance the spirit, strengthen the tendons and bones, and fortify the brain.

Footnotes:

1) Smashing fist is also commonly referred to as "crushing fist."

Section One

The Beginning Form
of Smashing Fist

At the beginning, make both hands in tight fists like the shell of a snail. Straighten the arms. The front left elbow has strength which goes inward and down, the rear right elbow has a strength which draws inward and back at the same time. Loosen both shoulders. Look at the middle section of the forefinger of the left hand. While stretching out the right hand, the left foot steps forward and the right hand goes straight forward passing close to the flank and about an inch away from the upper-side of the front fist. In the meantime, the left hand draws back close against the left flank near the heart and the right foot follows to step forward behind the front foot a distance of 4 to 5 inches. Both hands should be held at a level equal to the heart while going forward and drawing back.

Smashing Fist - Beginning Form

Section Two

The Changing Hand
of Smashing Fist

When starting again, the left foot goes forward as before. The left foot is in the front and the right foot follows at the back of the left, keeping a distance of 4 to 5 inches. The right-side form is like the left-side form. The left hand stretches straight forward away as the right hand did previously, meanwhile, the right hand draws back to the right flank near the heart as the left hand did previously. This form has the meaning of criss-crossing and inter-linking. The number of repetitions depends on the site. However, turning back should be performed after the stretching out of the right hand.

Smashing Fist - Changing Hand

Section Three

The Turning Back of Smashing Fist

When turning back, hook back the left foot 90 degrees as shown in the photograph. When starting to turn back, the right hand falls down with the heart side (palm) inward and then pierces up along the body from navel to mouth, as if supporting the chin. When turning back, the right leg and right hand move up at the same time. The distance between the elbow and knee is about 2 inches. The tiptoe of the right foot is outward and tilts up as the right leg is lifted. The in-step shouldn't be stretched. At this time, the right hand pierces out and stops as in the splitting fist. The right foot steps forward and is set down at an angle of 90 degrees. The left hand goes up and down with the right foot at the same time. In the meantime, the right hand draws back to the heart. All the fingers of both hands are open at this time as in the tearing motion expressed in the splitting fist. The left foot follows the right foot. The left tiptoe points to the outer shin bone of the right foot. The left heel lifts about an inch. Both legs cross like scissors. The eyes look at the root of the thumb and the tip of the forefinger of the front hand. This form is also known as "The Leopard Climbs the Tree Upside Down."

Smashing Fist - Turning Back

Section Four

The Smashing Fist

When walking back again, the right foot makes a pad-step forward like the step in the splitting fist. Both hands are in fists as before. The right hand and the left foot go forward at the same time as before. Turning back is also as before.

Smashing Fist Right and Left

Section Five

The Closing Form of Smashing Fist

When closing, come back to the original starting point, in the style of "Leopard Climbs the Tree Upside Down." The right hand and left foot go out and stop as before. Then, draw back the right foot so that it is easy to draw back the left foot. The foot falls in a 90 degree angle. The left foot draws back to form the scissors style stance. When the left foot draws back, the left hand goes straight forward, the right hand draws back to the heart at the same time. Both hands are in fists. During every scissors style stance, the left knee contacts tightly to the bent inner part of the right leg. There should not be any crevice in the crotch. Both legs contact each other tightly in an appropriate degree. The eyes look at the middle section of the forefinger of the front hand which is at the level of the heart.

Both shoulders and both hips should be closing in to the center to draw strength. Lift the top of the head as before. Keep the posture stable and then take a short rest.

Smashing Fist - Closing Form

Chapter Three

The Study of Drilling Fist (Zuan Quan)

鑽
拳

General Principles

The Study of Drilling Fist

Drilling fist belongs to water and has its *Qi* in the shape of running water. There is no small area it cannot reach. When drilling upward, it is like a spring spurting suddenly out of the ground. Its manner is like the top of the spring which flashes when turning over. It belongs to the kidney in the body and is drilling in boxing. This is why it is said that the drilling fist appears to flash and belongs to water. When the *Qi* is mild, the kidney is full, and when it is perverse, the kidney is empty. With an empty kidney, the clean *Qi* cannot come up and the dirty *Qi* cannot go down; the boxing will not be smooth and unhindered. This obstructs the generation of real strength and the dissolution of clumsy force. This should be recognized by practitioners.

Section One

The Beginning Form of Drilling Fist

When starting, both hands are in fists. First, the front foot makes a pad-step forward with an appropriate distance as in splitting fist. When stretching the hands, the heart side of the front hand is downward and that of the rear hand is upward. Draw back the left hand to the place between the heart and navel. The thumb of the left hand turns in, closing to the belly. The right hand goes out from the back of the left hand, its height should not exceed the elbow. The heart side of the right hand faces the eyes and stops at a distance of about a foot from the eyes. The right foot steps forward with the right hand. The distance between the two feet equals that in the splitting fist. The up and down movement of the hands and feet should coincide with each other. Both shoulders and hips draw strength and the waist sinks down as in the trinity (*San Ti*) form. The eye sight goes upward to look at the middle section of the forefinger.

Drilling Fist - Beginning Form

Section Two

The Changing Hands of Drilling Fist

When continuing, the wrist of the right fist twists with the strength moving outward. The heart side of the right fist faces down. The wrist of the left fist twists with the strength moving inward, its heart side faces up. The right foot makes a pad-step. The motions of both hands and feet are just like in the left-side form. The number of repetitions depends on the site. However, turning back should be accomplished when the left hand is stretched out (forward).

Drilling Fist - Changing Hands

Section Three

The Turning Back of Drilling Fist

When turning back, the left foot hooks back. When hooking back the left foot, the heel should twist with strength moving outward. The left fist should also hook back toward the mouth. The heart side faces down. The wrist twists outward and stops. The wrist of the right fist twists with the strength moving inward until the heart side of the fist faces upward. The fist then drills out as in the splitting fist. Both hands move up and down as before. The right foot moves up and down with the right hand at the same time. It is also like the left and right side *Yin* and *Yang* alternation style.

Drilling Fist - Turning Back

Section Four

The Closing Form of Drilling Fist

When closing, walk to the original place. The left hand and foot stop in front. When turning back, the motion of the hand and foot is just like the right side. The strength going up to the top of the head and that going down with the waist are the same as before. When closing, the left foot steps forward as before, but the right foot follows closely behind it. This is the same with the following-step of the closing form of splitting fist. Make the body stable and then take a short rest as before.

Drilling Fist - Closing Form

Chapter Four

The Study of Pounding Fist (Pao Quan)

炮
拳

General Principles

The Study of Pounding Fist

The pounding fist, belonging to fire, is the opening and closing of the *Qi*. It is like a shell shot out from a cannon and has the most intense property in the most vigorous style. In the body it belongs to the heart. In the boxing, it is pounding. This is why it is said that the pounding fist is like a cannon and belongs to fire. When its *Qi* is mild, it makes the heart nimble and dexterous. When its *Qi* is perverse, it makes the heart muddled and ignorant. When the boxing is mild, it makes the body comfortable. When the boxing is perverse, it makes the four limbs lose their coordination. This point should be carefully studied by practitioners.

Section One

The Beginning Form of Pounding Fist

When starting, do not move the body, the right hand pushes out first along the body and coincides with the left hand, and furthermore coordinates with the left foot to go forth. However, both hands should stretch out slowly, slanting downward. Then raise the right foot at the height of the left shin bone and stop it at the inner shin bone of the left foot without falling. Turn both hands into fists at the same time and draw them back to contact both sides of the lower abdomen. The heart side of both hands face upward. Raise the left foot with both hands at the same time. The right foot falls to the ground at the same time as well. When raising the left foot, it should be in close contact with the inner shin bone of the right foot. The body is also as in the *Yin* and *Yang* coordination form. The strength of the waist moves downward and holds stable.

Pounding Fist - Beginning Form

Section Two

The Stepping Forward of Pounding Fist

When stepping forward, the left hand pierces upward along the body to the center of the forehead and its elbow has its strength going down. The fist goes to the center of the forehead and the right hand comes to the side of the heart. At this time, the wrist of the left fist twists outward to its limit until the fist's heart faces outward and the fist back closely contacts the center of the forehead. When turning over the hands, they go straight out from the heart, this is the same with the smashing fist. The left foot steps forward with the right hand and right foot following. The distance between the feet is also the same as with the steps of the smashing fist. The left foot is in the front and the right foot is in the rear; the right hand is in the front and the left hand is at the top center of the forehead. Here is also the meaning of criss-crossing the body. The eyes look to the middle section of the forefinger of the front hand. The front fist is at the height of the heart. The motions of the hands and feet should be in coordination. Both shoulders should be relaxed and drawing strength. Here is the meaning of the "empty center."

Pounding Fist - Stepping Forward

Section Three

The Changing Hands of Pounding Fist

When changing hands, both wrists twist strength inward and fall down to the lower abdomen in close contact with it. The heart sides of the hands are upward. Both elbows are also in contact with both flanks. The left foot makes a pad-step forward at the same time. The foot should go out straight. Then the right foot steps forward slantingly to the right side of the shin bone of the left foot. This is the same with the left side form. The right hand pierces up to the center of the forehead and its wrist twists with strength outward with its heart side outward and back side in contact with the forehead. The elbow should have a strength going down when turning over. The left hand comes to the heart at the same time and goes out with the right foot. The left foot makes a following-step. This is also the same with the left-side form. Both shoulders draw strength as before. The number of repetitions depends on the site. However, turning back should be done after stretching out of the left hand and the right foot.

Pounding Fist - Changing Hands

Section Four

The Turning Back of Pounding Fist

When turning back, both hands fall down to the lower abdomen as before. The right foot hooks back as far as possible at the same time. The body turns to the left. The left foot raises in contact with the inner shin bone of the right foot and steps forward slantingly, followed by the right foot as before. The right hand goes out and the left hand pierces up and turns over with twisting strength as before.

Pounding Fist - Turning Back

Section Five

The Closing Form of Pounding Fist

The closing should be executed at the original starting place. The left hand and right foot are in front. The body also turns left. The motions of the hands and feet should be stable and without any flurry after stretching out. Then one may have a short rest.

Pounding Fist - Closing Form

Chapter Five

The Study of Crossing Fist (Heng Quan)

横

拳

General Principles

The Study of Crossing Fist

The crossing fist, belonging to earth and is the accumulation of *Qi*. It belongs to spleen in the body and is crossing fist in the boxing. Its shape is round and its property is solid. When the *Qi* is mild, the spleen and stomach are at ease; when it is perverse, the spleen becomes feeble and the stomach turns weak and hence the five viscera lose their harmony. When the boxing is mild, the internal organs are in harmony; when it is perverse, the internal *Qi* is strained. Strained internal *Qi* causes loss of the center which leads to a panic-stricken manner of the whole body. Thus all forms lose their shape. The *Qi* should be round and the strength should be mild. Everything grows from the earth. What is called crossing fist is like the ball and belongs to the earth. The old masters said that faith in the principle is just like the spleen in the body and the crossing fist in boxing. A person without faith fails in everything. A person with a hurt spleen loses the harmony of the five viscera. When crossing fist ceases to be mild, all forms loose their shape. Here different sentences have the same principle. Crossing fist is the important move in Xing Yi. Students should pay attention to it.

Section One

The Beginning Form of Crossing Fist

When starting, both hands are in fists, the left fist heart is upward and the right fist heart downward. When stretching out, the right fist back goes to the left fist back through the underside of the left elbow. At this time, the left hand holds the strength without moving. When the left foot stretches out, the right hand goes out slantingly in a complex manner with the left foot. Then the right foot makes a following step behind. The distance between both feet is like the following step in the pounding fist. When stepping forward, both hands exhibit twisting strength, the right wrist turns inward until the fist heart faces upward. The turning and twisting occurs at the same time when the fist pierces forward. There should not be any crooked strength.

The left wrist twists outward until the fist heart is downward and the fist back upward and simultaneously draws back to the right elbow. When separating both hands, it is as if tearing cotton that is hard to separate. Both shoulders enclose the center and secretly draw strength without manifesting it. It should not be urged by the mind and should be as natural as possible. At this time, the eyes look at the right fist heart. The arms form the shape of half the *Yin* and *Yang* symbols in the *Tai Ji* diagram. The front hand is at the height of the chest.

Crossing Fist - Beginning Form

Section Two

The Changing Hands of Crossing Fist

When changing hands, the left foot makes a pad step first, then steps forward slantingly to the right side like the step in the pounding fist. However, both hands are in the left-side form. The right hand gathers strength without moving. The left hand, with its back facing upward, goes to the right fist back through the underside of the right elbow. The left wrist twists inward and pierces straight forward until it reaches full extension and stops with the fist heart upward. The right wrist twists outward and draws back to the left fist back at the same time and stops with its fist back upward. When separating both hands, it is also like tearing cotton as mentioned previously. The arms form the shape of a half of the *Tai Ji* diagram. The hands and feet are in complex manner. The drawing strength and the direction of focus are as before. The number of repetitions depends on the site. However, turning back should be done after stretching out the left hand and right foot.

Crossing Fist - Changing Hands

Section Three

The Turning Back of Crossing Fist

When turning back, the right foot hooks back first and the heel twists outward with strength. The left hand holds strength and the body turns left. The right hand, with its back upward goes forward from the underside of the left elbow along the back side of the left arm. The left foot steps forward slantingly outward in coordination with the right hand. The separating strength in both hands is the same as before.

Crossing Fist - Turning Back

Section Four

The Closing Form of Crossing Fist

When closing, return to the original starting place, the left hand and right foot are in the front. The turning back form is also the same as above. After turning back, the right hand and left foot are in the front. The advancing and following-steps are also the same as before. Then stop.

Crossing Fist - Closing Form

Chapter Six

The Study of
Advancing and Retreating:
Linking the Five Fists

五拳合一進退連環學

General Principle

The Study of Advancing and Retreating: Linking the Five Fists

What is called "linking fist" is a style which combines the Wu Xing. The separate demonstration of Wu Xing is called Wu Xing boxing. Here it means "five key links." The combined demonstration of Wu Xing becomes "seven stars connecting one another." Here it means linking. In separation or combination there is always the actions of rising, drilling, falling, and overturning, of *Yin-Yang* and motion-rest. Whatever kind of rising, drilling, falling, and overturning it is, it involves the circulation of *Qi*. The rising, drilling, falling, and overturning are also the segments of the circulating *Qi*[1].

Zhong Rong[2] said that pleasure, anger, sorrow, and joy not having been developed fully is called "moderate;" while if they have been developed it is called "harmonious." In relation to boxing; rising, drilling, falling, and overturning not having been fully expressed is called moderate; while if they have been fully expressed it is called harmonious. What is called moderation is the foundation of Xing Yi boxing. What is called harmonious is the approach of Xing Yi boxing[3]. The composite of Wu Xing causes and improves moderation and harmony. Thus the heaven and earth have their proper position and generate everything. Understanding the composite of Wu Xing which causes and improves moderation and harmony, everything can be analyzed and realized.

The heaven is the great heaven. Humankind is a small heaven. The combination of the heaven and earth, *Yin* and *Yang*, can generate rain. The combination of *Yin* and *Yang* of fist and foot can form an integral unit. This is due to the *Qi* of *Yin-Yang*. The internal Wu Xing[4] should be in motion and the external Wu Xing should follow. Rest is the substance and the motion is the practice. To say that it is in rest, there is not any secret nature divulged; to say that it is in motion, there is not any trace to be seen. This is the case of motion and rest between discharge and non-discharge. It is called the moment of motion and rest. The old masters said that the one who recognizes the moment is the wisest[5]. So students should make a profound study on the three substances[6] in connection and of two-five[7] in combination.

Footnotes:

1) Rising, drilling, falling, and overturning all belong to the property of one *Qi*.

2) *Zhong Rong* is a classical book of Ru school, written by Zi Si, one of the students of Kong Zi (Confucious). (T)

3) The "approach" refers to the theories of the boxing art, its rules and laws. During practice one obeys the rules and laws and the practice becomes moderate and harmonious. The interior and exterior are identical. All things between the earth and sky can be understood accordingly.

4) The internal Wu Xing refers to the Lungs, Liver, Kidney, Heart, and Spleen. Because they exist inside the body they are called "Internal Wu Xing." The lung opens to the nose, the liver connects with the eyes, the kidneys connect with the ears, the heart connects with the mouth and tongue, the spleen connects with the lips. These are the external physical relationships of the five organs and are called the "External Wu Xing." Once motion starts in the interior, the external manifestation will accompany it. Once *Qi* circulates in the interior, the external forms can be harmonious and smooth. The smoothness of the external forms is the harmony of the spirit *Qi* in the interior. The correctness of the external forms moderates the emergence of *Qi* in the interior. This is the coordination of the interior and exterior.

5) Those who can detect the intention of the movement before the movement occurs can reach the extremely superior stage of practice.

6) *San Ti* means the three substances, i.e. the heaven, earth, and humankind.

7) Two refers to *Yin* and *Yang*, five refers to Wu Xing. Zhou Deng Yu's *Explanation of the Tai Ji Diagram* said that Wu Xing is the Yin and Yang in combination. *Yin* and *Yang* refers to one *Tai Ji*. *Tai Ji* originates from *Wu Ji*. The reality of *Wu Ji* forms the essentials of the two-five when combined.

Section One

The Linking Fist Beginning Form Smashing Fist Style

When starting, both hands turn into fists. The advances are the same with the form of smashing fist. It has the same principle of the straight battle array.

Splitting Fist - Beginning Form

Section Two

The Linking Fist Blue Dragon Coming Out of the Water

The retreat is the same as the scissors style described at the closing in the smashing fist. It has the same principle as the left wing of a troop.

Linking Fist - Blue Dragon Coming Out of the Water

Section Three

The Linking Fist Black Tiger Coming Out of its Cave

After the form above is the form of the "black tiger coming out of its cave." The right hand and right foot go out. The right foot should stretch out straight. The left foot makes a following-step in a slanting way. The inner-side shin bone of the rear left foot should be opposite of the heel of the front right foot. The right hand stretches out horizontally from the right flank and heart. The fist is the same with that in the smashing fist. The eyes look to the middle section of the forefinger of the right hand. The left wrist twists strength inward with its fist heart upward. In the meantime, both hands draw back at the same time to the right flank and stop there.

When both hands begin to draw, both shoulders enclose the center and draw strength backward. When stepping forward, both hips also enclose the center and draw strength backward. This style is called the "black tiger coming out of its cave." It has the same principle as the right wing of a troop.

**Linking Fist - Black Tiger
Coming Out of its Cave**

Section Four

The Linking Fist White Crane Spreading Wings

First, bring the right hand back below the heart, opposite the left fist. Both fist hearts are in contact with the abdomen. Then both wrists twist strength outward until both fist backs face inward. Lift both fists up slowly to the upper side of the forehead and then separate them from each other like a thread, with the right one moving forward and the left one moving backward, and stop respectively in front and at back opposite to each other at the shoulder level. The track of both fists is like an upper half circle. Then the left foot steps back and both fists fall down to the lower belly. Their track at this time is like the lower half circle. Both elbows at this time are in contact with both flanks. The left fist changes into a palm and the right fist sits down on its back in the left palm. The eyes look at both fists when they lift up and at the right fist when they fall down. The right foot draws back closing to the left foot when both hands fall down to the lower belly. Hold the right foot in a relatively straight manner contacting tightly with the inner shin of the left foot with its heel. The body should be in a three-fold stance. The waist should draw strength down. Both shoulders and hips draw strength as before. The head goes straight upward and the body should be stable. The eyesight goes forward. This style is like an army marching with both wings spreading. So it is called the white crane spreading wings.

Linking Fist - White Crane Spreading Wings

Section Five

The Pounding Form of Linking Fist

Changing into pounding fist, the right hand drills up to the central forehead. The wrist twists strength outward and the fist back is still close to the central forehead. In the meantime, the left hand drills up to the heart and then goes straight forward, the right foot steps forward and the left foot makes a following-step, then stops. This is like the practice of the single pounding fist, but here the stepping forward is going straight, not in a slanting way. In this form, both wings combine into one and make a straight advance. It presents a concentration of force, so it is called pounding fist.

Linking Fist - Pounding Form

Section Six

The Splitting Form of Linking Fist

Changing into the splitting fist, the left hand falls down to the belly along a half circular track as splitting in the splitting fist. The left foot steps back straight. The left hand drills up to the heart level along the body with its palm side inward. The right hand then splits straight forward and then downwards . The left hand then splits forward from the mouth. At this time, the right hand draws back from the underside of the left hand. Both hands split from each other as in the splitting fist. The right hand draws back to the right flank, at the same time, the right foot steps back to the rear side of the left foot. The distance between them is as in the splitting fist. The eyes look to the thumb root and the forefinger tip. Both shoulders and both hips release and draw strength. At this time, there is a coincidence of *Yin* and *Yang* in the body. The belly feels as though it is empty. This form has the meaning of being in the direction of metal. So it is called splitting fist.

Linking Fist - Splitting Form

Section Seven

The Wrapping Form of Linking Fist

The wrapping form is also called crossing fist. In this form, the middle, ring, and little fingers of both hands are curled in. The thumb and forefinger of both hands move straight out with strength. Both fist hearts draw strength covertly in coincidence with both shoulders. Then, the left hand falls down to the lower belly, the wrist wraps inward and the left elbow is close to the left flank. After this, the left hand drills up to the mouth, the wrist twists strength outward and stretches forward slantingly with twisting strength. When it goes to its utmost, the palm side turns downward. Though the arm stretches forward slantingly, the basic motion is out of the heart. When the left hand wraps inward, the left foot steps back to the front side of the right shin and contacts with the ground only with the toe, the heal is raised up. Then the left foot steps out with the left hand and goes to the original place. When the left foot is falling down, the right hand drills out from heart to mouth with its wrist wrapping strength inward. When it drills up, the palm side is upward and the forefinger stretches out horizontally at mouth level. When the right hand stretches out, the left hand draws back to the left flank with its heart side downward. The right foot makes a following step at the same time. This form is also staggered so as to perform both sides. The body is in three-fold shape. Its extent is that the lower belly sits on the hip of the left leg. This wrapping up style presents a round shape. It belongs to earth.

Linking Fist - Wrapping Form

Section Eight

The Leopard Climbing Tree Form of Linking Fist

Changing into the style of the "leopard climbing tree," the left foot makes a pad-step forward. Then the left hand and the right foot go forward at the same time. In the meantime, the right hand draws back to the right side of the heart with the left foot making a following step instantly. Both legs are in crisscross shape. Both hands are open. Both shoulders and both hips are drawing strength. All these should be done at the same time without any error. If there is any error, the internal *Qi* can't be mild and becomes clumsy. This clumsy *Qi* will hinder progress or success. While a leopard climbs a tree, it stretches out its claws. This is like the battle array with weapons stretching out preparing to fire. So it is called the "leopard climbing tree style."

Linking Fist - Leopard CLimbing Tree Form

Section Nine

The Smashing Form of Linking Fist

Changing into smashing form, the right foot makes a pad-step first, then the left foot steps forward at its utmost with the stretching out of the right hand. The left hand draws back to the left side of the heart with the right foot making a following step. The strength of both hands and feet and the distance between both feet are entirely the same with that in the smashing fist. After stopping, turn back. This is called the straight style. It has the meaning of advancing without rest.

Linking Fist - Smashing Form

Section Ten

The Turning Back Form of Linking Fist

The turning back is in the style of "leopard climbing tree upside down." It stops with the same posture as the turning back with crisscross legs in the smashing fist. This style has the meaning of getting success from an army which appears defeated.

Linking Fist - Turning Back

Section Eleven

The Repeating of the Linking Fist

At the beginning of repeating, the right foot makes a pad-step, the left foot steps forward with right hand stretching out. The style and the strength are just the same as in the first section through the tenth section.

Section Twelve

The Closing of the Linking Fist

The closing form is the same as in the smashing fist.

Linking Fist - Closing Form

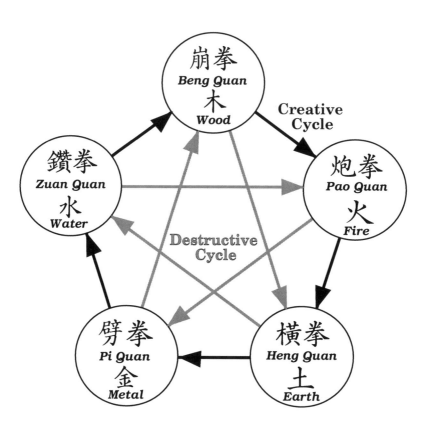

Chapter Seven

The Study of Wu Xing Pounding of the Creative and Destructive Five Fists

五拳生克五行炮學

General Principle

The Study of Wu Xing Casting of the Permuting Five Fists

The linking of the seven stars spoken of previously is the composite of five metals. It is the substance formed through the development of *Yin-Yang* and Wu Xing. This is the application of the creative and destructive Wu Xing. It is also called Wu Xing pounding.

The Wu Xing boxing practiced separately as described in the first part of chapter 6 is like self-cultivation, which means at the level of building up and taking care of oneself. While the Wu Xing boxing practiced in "linking" in the last part of Chapter 6 is like ruling one's family, which means at the level of building up and taking care of one's family. At this level, the principle of the Wu Xing boxing can be completely realized and put into application. The old masters said that metal style relates to splitting, wood style relates to smashing, water style relates to drilling, fire style relates to pounding, and earth style relates to crossing. Each of them has its own appropriate application. This is the principle of permutation which has the meaning of mutual creation and destruction between the five elements.

Section One

The Five Element Creative and Destructive Fist

This form is performed by two persons *A* and *B* cooperatively. At the beginning, both of them are in the trinity stance. *A* is upper hand and *B* is under hand. First, *B* steps forward and attacks with a smashing fist with his right hand. *A* slaps *B*'s right fist with his left hand and steps back with both feet, the left foot is still forward and the right hand is still at the right flank.

Section Two

The Five Element Creative and Destructive Fist

B steps forward and attacks with smashing fist again with the left hand. *A* makes a pad-step with the left foot with the tiptoe slanting outward and makes a drilling fist with the left hand, as in the splitting fist, to the outside of *B*'s left hand, and stops with fist heart inward. Next, he stretches out his right hand swiftly from the right flank to his own left hand and splits down toward *B*'s head and shoulder; at the same time, his right foot steps down to the rear outside of *B*'s left foot. In this way, the splitting fist breaks the smashing fist. This is why we say that metal restrains wood.

B　　　　　　　　　　　　　　　　　　　　**A**

Section Three

The Five Element Creative and Destructive Fist

B drills and turns with the left hand, turning the wrist outside and the left fist upward, and hits *A*'s heart with his right hand. Both feet stand still. This is pounding fist. Smashing fist belongs to wood and pounding fist to fire. Wood can produce fire, so smashing fist can change into pounding fist. As the pounding fist belongs to fire and fire restrains metal, the pounding fist can break the splitting fist.

B      **A**

Section Four

The Five Element Creative and Destructive Fist

A lifts up the right foot and draws back to the front side of his own left foot and makes a pad-step with the tiptoe slanting outward. The left fist falls down with rolling strength inward to press *B*'s right hand. The elbow is near the flank. At this time, *A* draws his right hand back swiftly to the right flank and his left foot steps forward to the inside of *B*'s right foot, the right fist drills out to *B*'s chin along his own body with the elbow closing to the flank and the fist heart upward. The eyes fall down on *B*'s eyes to see his changing. This is what we call" the drilling fist can break the pounding fist." Splitting fist belongs to metal and drilling fist belongs to water. Metal can produce water, so splitting fist can change into drilling fist. Water restrains fire, so drilling fist can break pounding fist.

B  **A**

Section Five

The Five Element Creative and Destructive Fist

B draws back his right hand to his right flank, in the meantime, his left hand pushes with slanting strength to the upper arm of *A*'s right elbow, both feet stand still. *B* uses *A*'s slanting strength. This is what we call "crossing fist can break drilling fist." Pounding fist belongs to fire and crossing fist belongs to earth. Fire produces earth, so pounding fist can change into crossing fist. Earth restrains water, so crossing fist can break drilling fist.

B  A

Section Six

The Five Element Creative and Destructive Fist

A draws back his right hand and attacks B's heart with his left hand, both feet stand still. This is what we call smashing fist. Drilling fist belongs to water and smashing fist belongs to wood, so drilling fist can change into smashing fist. Wood restrains earth, so smashing fist can restrain crossing fist.

B  A

Section Seven

The Five Element Creative and Destructive Fist

B slaps *A*'s left fist with his right hand and draws back his left hand and left foot to the back of the right foot, like the splitting fist style.

Section Eight

The Five Element Creative and Destructive Fist

A steps forward again and attacks with a right hand smashing fist.

B   A

Section Nine

The Five Element Creative and Destructive Fist

B slaps *A*'s right fist with his left hand again, and draws back his right hand and right foot as described previously.

Section Ten

The Five Element Creative and Destructive Fist

A steps forward and attacks again with a left hand smashing fist.

Section Eleven

The Five Element Creative and Destructive Fist

B drills out with the left fist, as in the single splitting fist, to the outside of *A*'s left hand from under the belly with the fist heart upward; then stretches out his right hand and advances his right foot. The way of splitting and advancing and the strength of each action are the same with the first form performed by *A*. This shows also that splitting fist breaks smashing fist. Its principle is that metal restrains wood.

B   A

Section Twelve

The Five Element Creative and Destructive Fist

A and *B* change their position with each other. Each of them performs what the other did before. This Wu Xing Permutation Boxing is practised repeatedly in this way. During this practice, the internal *Qi* runs to and fro without any break. After being versed in this practice and realizing its essence, one cultivates a wonderful feeling which cannot be described by words. The old masters said that the reality of *Tai Ji* is the essence of unity. This can also be used to describe the Wu Xing creative and destructive boxing.

Part Two

The Study of
the Xing Yi
Twelve Forms
Derived From
Heaven and Earth

形意天地生十二形學

Part II
The Study of the Xing Yi Twelve Forms Derived from Heaven and Earth

Everything is produced from *Yin-Yang* and *Wu Xing* and shaped with *Qi* by heaven[1]. This is the basic principle. The rule of heaven produces men and the rule of earth produces women. Thus exists the rule of humankind. Heaven is the big heaven, and men are the small heaven. The coincidence between *Yin-Yang* and the mutual promotion and destruction of Wu Xing being applied to the four limbs of our body give rise to Xing Yi boxing[2]. The basic principle, just like the unique *Qi*, has not a second. Things such as animals and plants get the partial *Qi* and thus have their partial principle. Humankind get the integral *Qi* and thus have their integral principle. Things get the partial *Qi*, however they can develop their property received from heaven and do what they can do. As for humankind, they get the integral *Qi* from heaven and earth and have the integral principle, but they almost always hold only a part of the principle and cannot carry out the possibility of researching and drawing lessons from the principle of all things on earth to enrich themselves[3].

Things can imitate humankind, but most times humankind cannot realize the principle of all things on the earth to fulfill their own life[4]. Now, if we can learn and practice the boxing of twelve styles (twelve animals) and combine the theory and practice together, we cannot only enhance our knowledge level and mental ability, but also promote our health day after day[5]. So it is worthy for students to exert their strength in the twelve style boxing training.

The twelve styles represent twelve kinds of animals that come from the heaven and earth[6]. They are dragon, tiger, monkey, horse, water lizard, chicken, sparrow hawk, swallow, snake, tai bird[7], eagle, and bear. All these creatures are formed from the *Qi* of heaven and earth and live based on their own principle. These twelve styles can represent the principle of all styles on earth and thus become the guiding principle of all styles. Therefore, to learn the twelve style boxing one can reach to the principle of all things derived from heaven and earth.

Footnotes:

1) Heaven produces the ten thousand things with the essence of *Yin-Yang* and *Wu Xing*. The formation of *Qi* and the theory of interaction between *Yin* and *Yang* exist within it.

2) In practice of the boxing skill one strives to maintain the mutual existence of *Yin* and *Yang* and the harmonization of the *Wu Xing*. It was mentioned previously that moderateness is the basis of Xing Yi Quan, therefore, Xing Yi is developed from moderateness.

3) This integral *Qi* is the congenital *Qi*. The principle refers to the interaction between *Yin* and *Yang*.

4) All things are generated by the *Qi* of heaven and earth. There are advantages and disadvantages respectively. Nothing is fully complete. However, everything begins with its pre-heaven nature.

5) The human being is influenced by the *Qi* and theory of both the heaven and earth. If one theory is emphasized without full comprehension of the nature and characteristics of the ten thousand things, you risk your own life. This responsibility must be taken by the human being himself.

6) During the practice of boxing, through experience, the human being can understand the nature of the animals in the twelve styles and adopt their advantages for personal application. In this way one is able to build up the morality of the interior and build the body externally.

7) The tai bird is a mythical animal.

Chapter One

The Study of Dragon Form (Long Xing)

龍
形

General Principle

The Study of Dragon Form

The dragon style has the "descending dragon" posture and the "hiding dragon ascending to heaven" posture. Here lies the method of circulating internal *Qi* through the bones[1]. Dragon belongs to *Yin*. Originally dragon belonged to *Yang*, but it belongs to *Yin* in the boxing. Practicing the dragon style can promote the internal fire going down. *Dan Shu* said that the dragon can quench fire. Clouds belong to dragon and become the emblem of the dragon. It is called dragon style in the boxing. In this style, the strength begins from the point *Cheng Jiang*[1]. It connects with the *Qi* of the tiger style[3]. For these two styles, one is forward and ascendant, the other is backward and descendant. The boxing performed with mild *Qi* can promote the internal fire going down and performed with erroneous *Qi* will cause the body to be burnt in the *Yin* fire. In the later case, the body will be with stagnation of the circulation of vital energy and a loss of flexibility. Students can realize this point through profound study and practice.

Footnotes:

1) Since the dragon includes ascending, descending, extending, and contracting, one must start from the contracting of the bones and tendons. Once contracting, once expanding, once extending, once retracting, then one may have endless changes.

2) The *Cheng Jiang* is a point at the center of the indentation between the lower lip and the chin. This point lies on the *Ren* meridian. (T)

3) The beginning of the dragon's energy is the *Cheng Jiang* point. This *Qi* goes down. The *Qi* of the tiger form begins at the *Chang Qiang* point, between the genitals and anus, and moves up. These forms complete the circulation of the *Ren* and *Du* meridians.

Section One

The Beginning Form of Dragon

The dragon style starts from trinity (*San Ti*). First, the left tiptoe twists outward, the left foot makes a pad-step crosswise forward with foot heart suspended. The right foot turns straight and stands on tiptoe with the heel suspended. Both hands move as in splitting fist, the right hand stretches out and the left hand draws back. Both hips enclose to the center and relax. The body bends over with the lower belly on the left leg. The style looks like a dragon crouching down. The eyes look to the forefinger of the front hand which is at the level aligned with the heart. The waist draws strength down. Both shoulders relax and draw strength as before. Hold the posture stably.

Dragon - Beginning Form

153

Section Two

The Changing Form of Dragon

When changing, the right hand draws back and drills out like splitting fist. The left hand stretches out. Both hands are still like splitting fist. Both legs exchange their positions. The left leg draws backward like the right foot style, and the right leg steps forward like the left foot style. In the meantime, both hands are in their motion. It has the meaning of a flying dragon ascending to the heaven. While descending, the four limbs should be in coherence with one another. The body has its ascending style, but it should not stand up when changing. The head is always vertically straight and draws strength upward. Hold the form stably and prepare for another change.

Dragon - Changing Form

Section Three

The Second Changing Form of Dragon

During the second change, the raising and falling down of both hands, the exchanging of both legs, the relaxing and drawing strength of both shoulders and both hips are still as before. But when drilling out the hands, the eyesight goes upward following the hand, the chin protrudes forward and draws strength upward. This motion is based on the principle that the channel *Ren* begins from the point *Cheng Jiang*. The number of repetitions depends on the site.

Dragon - Second Changing Form

Section Four

The Closing Form of Dragon

The closing form comes back to the left form. The right hand and left foot are in the front. Make it stable and then draw back the right hand, the left hand still goes out, so as to come back to trinity (*San Ti*).

Dragon - Closing Form

Chapter Two

The Study of Tiger Form (Hu Xing)

虎形

General Principle

The Study of Tiger Form

There are different forms of "lying tiger leaving its cave" and the "hunting tiger catching its captive." In this style, the clean *Qi* of the kidney water goes up in the abdomen. *Dan Shu* says that the tiger goes up with ascending water. This has the same meaning. Wind always follows the tiger and becomes the symbol of it. It is the tiger style in the boxing. *Ten Wei*, i.e. *Chang Qiang*[1] cannot be seen while going up and down. This describes the manner of a tiger lying and sitting in, and going in and out of its cave. When the boxing is performed mildly, clean *Qi* ascends and the brain is replenished. When the boxing is performed adversely, the dirty *Qi* cannot descend and all channels are blocked. Medical books point out that *Du* Meridian is the source of all channels. This means that the free circulation of *Du* Meridian makes all channels clear. Students should understand this principle of the tiger style so as to clear all channels.

The Trinity (*San Ti*) Posture

Footnotes:

1) The *Chang Qiang* is a point on the *Du* meridian located between the coccyx and the anus.

Section One

The Beginning Form of Tiger

The starting form is the trinity posture. First, stretch out both left and right hands slanting them down slightly. The body draws strength with the coincidence of *Yin* and *Yang* without any shifting. The left foot makes a pad-step. Then the right foot steps forward. The right foot crosses the left foot with a distance of one or two feet. When the right foot has not yet fallen down on the ground, the left foot lifts up and shifts close to the right shin. In the meantime, both hands brush back to the lower abdomen and turn into fists with each fist heart upward. Both elbows lean tightly on the flanks. The waist draws strength down. The drawing down strength of the waist is the main point when brushing, lifting, ascending, and descending, or the body cannot be light. The drawing upward strength of the head and the drawing downward strength of the waist are in accordance with the internal *Qi* concentrating at the *Dan Tian*. Make this stance stable. While performing this style, the body shifts swiftly forward with the drawing strength of the main body directed inward. Whether the step is far or near, it is not a jumping step.

Tiger - Beginning Form

Section Two

The Advancing Form of Tiger

The left foot stretches out and steps forward slantingly. The right foot makes a following-step as that in the pounding fist. Both hands drill upward to the chin, with turning at the same time, so that both wrists twist strength outward. Then both palms spring forward. The "tiger's mouth" of both hands are at the level of the heart. Both shoulders draw strength outward and backward. The left foot steps forward in a straight manner at the same time with the hands. The right foot makes a following-step as that in the pounding fist. Both eyes look to the center between both hands. Hold the form stable.

Tiger - Advancing Form

Section Three

The Changing Form of Tiger

Changing from left to right form, the left foot, in a straight manner, makes a pad-step as that in the pounding fist. In the mean time, both hands fall down to the lower abdomen as in the splitting fist. The difference between them is that both hands fall down here but only one hand falls down in the splitting fist. The motion of the feet is the same in both styles. Both eyes look to the right side. The eyes should not tilt up or fall down. There is a triangle formed by the body, the ground, and the eyesight. They are the shorter and longer sides of the triangle and the base respectively. The eyesight is the hypotenuse. The length of this hypotenuse should be so appropriate that the eyes are not tilting up or falling down. In this way, the floating fire cannot occur.

Section Four

The Changing Form of Tiger

Advancing again, the steps are the same as the pounding fist. The motion of both hands is the same as in the left form. The number of repetitions depends on the case. However, turning back should be executed after the right form. The right foot is in the front.

Tiger - Changing Form

Section Five

The Turning Back Form of Tiger

Turning the left side around, hooking in the right foot and stepping forward, all these are the same as in the pounding fist. When hooking in the right foot, both hands fall down to the lower abdomen. Then both hands spring forward with the advancing left foot. Advancing forward again is as described previously.

Tiger - Turning Back

163

Section Six

The Closing Form
of Tiger

The closing begins from the right side. The right foot is in the front. After stopping, the turning back and stepping forward, springing forward of both hands, all these are the same as described in the turning back form. After turning back, make the form stable before resting.

Chapter Three

The Study of Monkey Form (Hou Xing)

猴形

General Principle

The Study of Monkey Form

The monkey is the most exquisite of animals. It has the methods of saving energy and of jumping over the mountains. It corresponds to the heart in the body and to the monkey style in the boxing. Performing this style mildly, the heart and mind are quiet and stable, style and appearance are proper and fine. If it is performed erroneously, the heart and mind are confused and unstable, style and appearance become discordant and the limbs will be in disorder. Men Zi[1] said that the heart is the root which loads the change of feeling appearing in the face, spreading to the back, and going through the limbs[2]. Here it means the internal *Qi*. The moving technique of a monkey cannot be compared with the motion of a man. But through strict training according to its principle, man can concentrate his mind and lighten his body[3]. Students should not neglect these special effects.

Footnotes:

1) Men Zi (Mencius), 372-289 B.C., was a thinker, statesman, and educationist in the time of the warring states. His work *Men Zi* is one of the classical books of the Ru school. (T)

2) If the heart *Qi* of the organs in the abdomen is correct, then the complexion will be good and the movements of the limbs will be balanced and coordinated. This quote comes from Mencius. The original text reads: "The nature of the gentleman includes benevolence, righteousness, propriety and knowledge. The root is the heart, its activity will be visible in the complexion and will pass through the back to the extremities. Although the extremities cannot speak, they will manifest the meaning.

3) Although this form is hard to learn, if one comprehends deeply and practices diligently, pondering carefully the nature of this animal, not only will one be able to cultivate its spirit, but the body will become light.

Section One

The Keeping of the Seal Form of Monkey

Trinity is the starting point. Make it stable. Then the left foot lifts up, steps to the right side, and makes a pad-step with twisting strength outward. The left hand falls down to the lower abdomen. Then the left hand drills out as that in the splitting fist. The body, following the left foot, turns left. The right foot steps forward in front of the left foot with the toes hooking strength inward. At this time, the body faces southwest or northeast depending on the starting point. If it starts from the north, the body faces northeast. Then the left foot steps back behind the right foot at the same time with the left hand. Then the right hand stretches out from above the left hand. This form is the same as that in the splitting fist.

Monkey - Keeping of the Seal Form

Section Two

The Dragging the Rope Form of Monkey

First, the left foot steps back at its utmost and makes a pad-step. The right foot steps on the ground and pulls to the left foot with its tiptoe on the ground and its heel lifted up. The heel of the right foot is opposite the left shin. The body is in three-fold posture as in the photograph. The right hand draws back to the lower abdomen with its elbow tightly in contact with the flank. The left hand stretches out to the front of the mouth with its hand back upward. The distance between the hand and the mouth is two or three inches. Both hands are like eagle's claws in grasping. The five fingers are spread. The elbows are in contact with the flank. Both hips are closing to the center. The *Ten Wei* and both hips draw back to their utmost. The head goes forward and upward with strength and remains stable.

Monkey - Dragging the Rope Form

Section Three

The Climbing the Rod Form of Monkey

At first, the right foot makes a pad-step forward. The left hand stretches out straight. Then stretch out the right hand and step with the left foot. The left hand draws back to the left side of the heart, then stretch out the left hand and lift up the right leg. The root of the thigh is in contact with the lower abdomen. The tiptoe of the right foot tilts up. After a short stop, the right hand stretches out and the right foot falls down. In the meantime, the left hand draws back again. The motion of the limbs should be tidy. This style is the same with that of the splitting fist. Make it stable and then change.

Monkey - Climbing the Rod Form

Section Four

The Keeping the Seal Form of Monkey

First the right foot twists strength outward. The right hand falls down to the lower abdomen as in the left form and then drills up. The body turns right following the right foot. The left foot steps forward toward the right foot and hooks inward. At this time, the body faces northwest. Then stretch out the left hand. It is like the left side of the splitting form. All motions are just the same as the left form. The number of repetitions depends on the case. The turning back style can begin from either the left or right form.

Monkey - Keeping the Seal Form

Section Five

The Turning Back Form
of Monkey

When turning back, if the facing direction is northwest, the body turns left and faces southwest. The motions are the same with those performed in the left and right forms.

Monkey - Turning Back Form

Section Six

The Closing Form
of Monkey

The closing place should be the original starting place. The motions are the same as in the left and right forms. Make the posture stable and then rest.

Chapter Four

The Study of Horse Form (Ma Xing)

General Principle

The Study of Horse Form

The horse is the most righteous animal. Running fast and righteousness to its master are its two specialties[1]. It is the consciousness in the body. This consciousness is from the heart. In the boxing, it is the horse style. When it is performed mildly, the consciousness is stable with gentle respiration. If it is performed erroneously, the consciousness is unstable with strained respiration, thereby one will become clumsy in the limbs. The old masters said that an honest consciousness produces proper mind[2]. Proper mind leads to perfect assurance. This makes the strength in the boxing faultless and exact[3]. Students should pay attention to this reasoning.

Footnotes:

1) If the horses reins are released and no one controls the horse, the horse itself will find its way back home. This means that the horse can be trusted.

2) This means to know the principle, but not completely. Only when you are empty can you contain. One must understand this principle in order to research to the highest level.

3) The intent comes from the heart. If honesty is from the sincerity of the heart one will naturally be correct, the principle will be correct, and one will not fool himself or others. Then

The Trinity (*San Ti*) Posture

power will be issued appropriately. These sentences come from *The Great Learning*. "The essence of the teaching is to follow the correct principles without deviating from the proper method. Then one will naturally understand."

174

Section One

The Beginning Form
of Horse

The horse style starts from the trinity. The right foot makes a pad-step forward and steps down in a ninety degree angle with the forward direction. Both hands turn into fist. Both wrists draw strength inward with the fist heart upward. Both shoulders relax and draw strength. Don't draw back the left arm. Keep it with strength. Next, the right hand stretches out passing under the left hand. At this time, both fist hearts are upward. When both hands are separating from each other, the right hand pushes forward with strength. The left hand draws back with strength and stops at the heart. Both wrists twist strength outward until both fist backs are upward. Both fists are opposite each other. The right foot and right hand go forward to their utmost. The left foot makes a short following step but shouldn't be too close to the front foot. Both eyes look to the root section of the forefinger of the front hand. Both arms are in a shape like the two halves of the *Tai Ji* diagram. Both elbows rise horizontally as in the photo. Both shoulders relax outward and draw strength. Make it stable.

Horse - Beginning Form

Section Two

The Changing Form
of Horse

In the changing form, the twisting strength and pad-step, the opposition of both hands, the drawing strength of both shoulders, and the falling down point of the eyes, are all the same as performed in the left form. The number of repetitions depend on the case. However, the turning back should begin from the left form.

Horse · Changing Form

Section Three

The Turning Back Form of Horse

When turning back, the body turns right following the right hand. Both hands and feet are the same as in the splitting fist. The following left and right forms are all the same as before.

Section Four

The Closing Form
of Horse

Turning back at the original starting place. Perform the right form and make it stable. Then rest.

Chapter Five

The Study of Water Lizard Form (Tuo Xing)

鼉
形

General Principle

The Study of Water Lizard Form

The water lizard[1] is the most flexible animal in the water. It has the ability to float. It belongs to kidney in the human body. It can clear up the heart fire, eliminate edema and distention, and dispel indigestion. In the boxing, it belongs to the water lizard style. This style can activate the tendons and sinews of the whole body and dissipate the clumsy force. When it is performed mildly, the weak tendons and bones can be strengthened, the frail sinews can be enforced, the shortened tendons can be extended, and the slackened tendons can be adjusted. This means that one who obeys heaven is preserved. If it is performed erroneously, the strength at the limbs, shoulders, and hips will be constrained and this will cause the body to be inflexible. Thus it is hard to get mutual affinity between the inside and outside of the body like that achieved by the water lizard between its body and the water and hence it can float on the water surface.

Footnotes:

1) This form is sometimes also called "water strider" or "alligator."

Section One

Beginning the Left Wrapping Form of Water Lizard

The form starts from the trinity. The left hand is wrapped upward toward the chin. The hand heart is upward. The elbow contacts tightly with the flank. The left foot draws back to the front of the right shin simultaneously with the movement of the left hand.

Note: The photograph shown below is demonstrating the right side. The left side, as described above, is the same posture only in reverse.

Water Lizard - Beginning Left Wrapping Form

Section Two

The Left Wrapping Form
of Water Lizard

The left hand stretches out slantingly from the mouth with the left foot at the same time. It is the same with that in the wrapping form of the linking fist. When the left hand is falling down, stretch out the right hand.

Water Lizard - Left Wrapping Form

Section Three

The Right Wrapping Form of Water Lizard

The right hand wraps with strength and drills out from the right flank to the mouth and the elbow is in contact with the flank. The right hand drills forward about a foot from the mouth. The hand heart is still upward. This is the same as in the wrapping of the right hand of the linking form boxing[1]. In conjunction with the motion of the right hand, the right foot steps to the shin of the left foot. The right foot seems as though it is in contact with the left shin and should not fall down on the ground.

Footnotes:

1) This movement is the same as section seven in the linking form, however, in the linking form the hand moves out in a straight line and in this form the hand moves laterally. The *jing* is the same.

**Water Lizard -
Right Wrapping Form**

183

Section Four

The Changing Form
of Water Lizard

The right hand and the right foot stretch forward slantingly with turning strength.   It is the same as with the left form.

Water Lizard - Changing Form

Section Five

The Changing Again Form of Water Lizard

Stretch out the left hand and foot as in the right wrapping form. The eyes look to the forefinger. The separation and coming together of both hands are connected together without any break and in coincidence with the waist. All motions are led by the unique *Qi*. It is as though all rivers come from the same source. The number of repetitions depends on the case.

Section Six

The Turning Back Form of Water Lizard

In turning back, when the right hand and foot stretch out crossingly, the right foot does not fall down but hooks back instantly. The body turns left following the left hand which stretches out as in wrapping up. The right foot follows. The left and right form are as before.

Section Seven

The Closing Form of Water Lizard

The closing is like the turning back. All motions of both styles are the same. Rest should be taken only after making the posture stable.

Chapter Six

The Study of Chicken Form (Ji Xing)

General Principle

The Study of Chicken Form

The cock is the most useful among animals for mankind, it announces the dawn. It has the ability of standing on one leg, the sternness of shaking the feathers, and the bravery to fight. The cock is the beginning of the moving of *Yin* in human body, and is corresponds to the *Xun Gua* in Ba Gua. It also corresponds to wind in heaven, to respiration in human body, and to the chicken style in boxing. It can raise the strength from the heel, drop the air from the head, and spread the vital *Qi* in whole body. When the chicken style is performed mildly, there is no deficiency in the brain above and no pain in the legs below. If it is performed erroneously, it will promote an inefficient brain, blurred eyes and ears, and clumsy limbs. These points should not be neglected by students.

Footnotes:

1) *Xun* is one of the eight diagrams in Ba Gua and represents wind. (T)

The Trinity (*San Ti*) Posture

Section One

The Golden Cock Stands on One Leg Form of Chicken

The starting point is trinity. The right hand stretches out from under the left hand. The waist, hips, and shoulders follow the right hand. The right leg bends its knee and lifts up its heel. The right hand draws back with its elbow in contact with the flank. Then the right foot steps forward to the front of the left foot. The right foot should not step down to the ground. Its height should be in parallel with the left shin. Then the right hand draws back from above the left hand and the left hand goes out from under the right hand. Both hands are in palms. The left foot lifts up to the right shin when the right foot steps down. The motions of both hands and feet should be unified. The waist should draw strength down. At this time, both hips and shoulders draw strength in the way of coincidence between *Yin* and *Yang*. The right leg is bent. The left hand pushes strength slantingly down and forward. The thumb root of the right hand leans on the side of the navel. The eyes look to the forefinger tip and the thumb root of the left hand. The body seems to be bound with a rope. Make the posture stable and then go forward.

**Chicken - Golden Cock
Stands on One Leg**

Section Two

The Latter Golden Cock Stands on One Leg Form of Chicken

Step forward but keep both hands stable without any motion. The right elbow leans on the flank. The left hand pushes strength at its utmost. Then the left foot steps forward at its utmost and down on the ground. Then the right foot steps forward at its utmost too. But when the right foot has not yet stepped down on the ground, the left foot lifts up and leans on the right shin. Then make it stable. The steps of this style are the same with the first step of the tiger style. The difference of this style from others is that the left hand pushes strength and keeps it still and the right hand is leaning on the side of the navel without any motion.

Section Three

The Golden Cock Pecking Rice Form of Chicken

The left hand keeps the strength still. The right hand rolls up into a fist and goes forward as in the smashing fist. The left foot steps forward in a straight manner with the right hand. But the left hand does not draw back, it hooks on the right wrist. The right foot then follows swiftly to the left foot as in the smashing fist. The eyes look to the middle section of the right forefinger. Both shoulders draw strength backward. Both hips enclose the center. Make the form stable.

Chicken - Golden Cock Pecking Rice

Section Four

The Former Golden Cock Shakes its Feathers Form of Chicken

Hold up both hands in front of the chest. Both hand hearts face inward. The left hand is inside and the right is outside. The distance between the hands and the chest is about two or three inches. Both elbows draw strength downward. Both shoulders draw strength downward and outward. The body seems to be bound with a rope. Both arms are in a cross. The right foot draws back. Thus both legs are in a shape of riding a horse. Both heels twist strength outward stealthily. Both knees hook in with strength stealthily too. Both roots of the thighs draw strength inward and open strength outward stealthily at the same time.

Chicken - The Former Golden Cock Shakes its Feathers

Section Five

The Latter Golden Cock Shakes its Feathers Form of Chicken

Separate both hands in a way that the right fist bores up along the front central line to the forehead and then turns over as the turning-over hand in the pounding fist; at the same time, the left fist draws strength downward and backward to the rear side of the left flank with its fist heart backward as in the drawing hand in the splitting fist. Both feet turn into smooth form as in the photograph. The body twists strength following the right arm to the heart opposite the right knee and tiptoe. At this time, the eyes look to the root section of the right forefinger along the right hand. Both shoulders open strength outward.

Chicken - The Latter Golden Cock Shakes its Feathers

Section Six

The Golden Cock Stands Up on a Frame Form of Chicken

Both fists turn into palms. The right wrist twists strength inward until the hand heart is inward, then stretches right away toward the underside of the left arm at its utmost with its wrist leaning tightly on the left flank. The left hand closely contacts with the body and stretches right away toward the right shoulder in conjunction with the movement of the right hand. The body and both arms seem to be bound by a rope and drawn by two persons holding the ends from opposite directions. Both shoulders draw strength downward with stealthy opening strength outward. The body is in three-fold form with coincidence of *Yin* and *Yang*. In the meantime, the left foot steps forward to the front of the right foot. The right foot lifts up swiftly when the left foot has not yet stepped down on the ground and leans tightly on the left shin when the left foot falls down on the ground. The motions of both hands and feet should be unified. The waist draws strength downward. The eyes look forward along the left hand. Make the form stable.

Chicken - The Golden Cock Stands Up on a Frame Form

Section Seven

The Golden Cock Announces the Dawn Form of Chicken

The right hand lifts up from the downside to the level of the top of the head following the track of a half circle. The eyes look to the end section of the right forefinger following the right hand. The left hand draws to the rear side of the left flank with the right hand as that in the splitting fist. The right foot steps forward with the right hand. Both legs and feet are the same as in the splitting fist. Both shoulders draw an opening strength forward and backward and both roots of the thighs do the same too. At this time, the body is like a cubic square which seems to be drawn from four directions with ropes at the same time. In the body, there is a feeling of emptiness like the vault of heaven. Out of the body, it is the vast square of the ground. This is what is meant by "round inside and square outside."

Chicken - The Golden Cock Announces the Dawn

Sections Eight Through Twelve

Section 8   The Splitting Fist Form of Chicken

The right hand keeps strength above. The right foot makes a pad-step. The left hand and foot go out again as in the splitting fist, but the right hand does not draw back and the left hand is a little bit higher when stretching out.

Section 9   The Splitting Fist Form of Chicken

After the former section, there are two splitting fists of the chicken style. The changing should be after the splitting of the right hand.

Section 10   The Golden Cock Standing on One Leg Form of Chicken

After changing the form, the right hand goes down and drills again. The left hand goes out as in the splitting fist, but the right foot draws back to the left foot when the right hand drills out. The left foot lifts up close to the right shin when the right foot is falling down.   The motions of the four limbs should be unified.   When going back to the original place, it is the golden cock standing on one leg stance.   Make it stable.

Section 11   The Golden Cock Pecking the Rice Form of Chicken

Change and do the golden cock pecking the rice form again. The number of repetitions depends on the case.

Section 12 The Closing of the Cock Style

The closing is at the original place. The stance is the splitting fist with the left hand in front.   The closing is as in the splitting fist. Make it stable before rest.

Chapter Seven

The Study of Sparrow Hawk Form (Yao Xing)

General Principle

The Study of Sparrow Hawk Form

The sparrow hawk has the method of drawing in its wings, the ability of penetrating into the forest, and the skill of turning over. In the body the sparrow hawk style can gather together the *Qi* of heart. In the boxing, it can shrink the body. When it is performed mildly, the prenatal *Qi* can be collected into the *Dan Tian*, the body can go up and down compactly and swiftly. This is what the old masters said when a bird flew with its wings drawn in. If it is performed erroneously, the heart is exerted, the internal *Qi* goes astray, and the body is in restraint. Through strict training of this style, one can go up as the birds fly with its wings drawn in and go down as the water flows fluidly down stream.

Section One

The Shrinking Form of Sparrow Hawk

The starting is the trinity posture. Both hands are in fists. The right fist goes to the underside of the left hand with its fist heart upward. The left wrist twists strength inward with its fist heart upward. The left foot makes a pad-step in a straight manner. The right foot steps forward also. When the right foot goes before the left foot one to two feet and has not yet fallen down to the ground, the left foot lifts up and moves closely to the right shin. The motions of the four limbs should be unified. The stepping forward in this style is as the first step in the tiger style. Make it stable. This is called the "shrinking of the sparrow hawk" of the sparrow hawk style.

Sparrow Hawk - Shrinking Form

Section Two

The Flying into the Forest Form of Sparrow Hawk

Stepping forward, both hands change into pounding fist. The right hand drills and turns upward and the left hand stretches forward. These movements are executed as in the pounding fist, but the left foot steps forward and the right foot remains stable. Make it stable. This style is called the "flying into the forest form of the sparrow hawk" and also called the "pounding fist with smooth steps."

Sparrow Hawk - Flying into the Forest Form

Section Three

The Penetrating into the Sky Form of Sparrow Hawk

The right arm twists inward with its wrist and elbow. The right fist heart is upward. The left wrist twists inward and the left fist heart is upward too. The right hand stretches out through the inside of the left wrist along the level of the shoulder. The left fist moves to the back of the right elbow as if to stroke the sleeves. The left fist heart turns downward. The left elbow leans tightly on the heart. The right foot and the right hand go forward at the same time. The motions of the limbs should be unified. This style is in general as the left form of the drilling fist. The eyes look to the middle section of the right forefinger. Make it stable. This style is called "penetrating into the sky" of the sparrow hawk.

Sparrow Hawk - Form

Section Four

The Turning Over Form of Sparrow Hawk

Turning back, the right hand bends back to the left shoulder passing in front of the eyes. In the meantime, the right foot hooks in its tiptoe. The left hand draws a circle along the body downward and then forward from under the right elbow. The right hand draws back to the rear side of the right flank at the same time with the left hand. Both fists separate opposite each other front and back. This stance is like holding a gun at the middle horizontal level. After the right foot hooks back, the left foot lifts up and leans to the right shin and then goes out at the same time with the left hand. The motions of the body and the feet are the same with that in the splitting fist, however, the body is a little bit lower. The eyes look to the middle section of the forefinger of the front hand. Make it stable. This style is called the "turning over" of the sparrow hawk.

Sparrow Hawk - Turning Over Form

Section Five

The Shrinking Form
of Sparrow Hawk

Step forward again. The motions are just the same as the shrinking form of the sparrow hawk in section one. The number of repetitions depends on the case.

Sparrow Hawk - Shrinking Form

Section Six

The Closing Form
of Sparrow Hawk

When closing, go back to the original place and turn back as in the "turning over" of the sparrow hawk (section four).   Make the posture stable and then rest.

Chapter Eight

The Study of Swallow Form (Yan Xing)

燕形

General Principle

The Study of Swallow Form

The swallow is the most flexible of birds. It has the special way of taking the water. It can draw the water of kidney upward to meet the fire of the heart in the body[1]. The *Yi Jing*[2] said that water and fire have been in harmonious proportion. The Ru school[3] said that the real primeval internal *Qi* has been restored[4]. So this style can activate the *Qi* of the waist in the boxing. Besides, the swallow has also the jumping flexibility. When the style is performed mildly, the brain is excited and full with spirit and energy. Hence the brain is strengthened. If the style is performed erroneously, the waist becomes dull and the body becomes sluggish and heavy. Thus the internal *Qi* in the body is in a stagnant way. Students should take notice of this point.

Footnotes:

1) The kidney belongs to water, the kidney water moves up to combine with the heart. The heart belongs to fire. The heart fire descends to combine with the kidney. One rising, one falling, moving without end. When upper and lower unite, then one is healthy.

2) The *Yi Jing* is a famous book which first appeared between the Ying and Zhou Dynasties, i.e. in time of about 1200 B.C. According to research, the contents of the book have accumulated through time. It is said that the Ba Gua diagram was invented by Fu Xi and developed into 64 diagrams with 384 Yaos by Zhou Wen Wan. The diagrams including Guas and Yaos in the book are a set of special signals representing each side of nature and imitating its principles of changes. (T)

3) The Ru school is a school of thought, members of which worship the doctrine of Kong Zi (Confucious). (T)

4) The pre-heaven (pre-birth) *Qi* is the real *yuan Qi* (original Qi). After training one recovers the real *Qi* and is not harmed by impure *Qi*.

Section One

The Beginning Form
of Swallow

Begin from the trinity posture. The right hand stretches out from the underside of the left hand and draws back to the forehead. The stance of the limbs and the body are the same with the style of the golden cock shaking the feathers. The body twists back and faces backward. The lower abdomen is on the right thigh. Hold the posture.

Swallow - Beginning Form

Section Two

The Drawing Water Form
of Swallow

The body twists to the front again. When twisting, the body should not move sideways and have to twist back with the drawing strength at its utmost. This is just like the turning back of the tip of a Chinese writing brush in calligraphy. The body seems to be turning back from the side, but the internal *Qi* and strength should not be with any intention of moving sideways. The left hand stretches straight forward in coincidence with the body. The left wrist twists inward until the hand heart is upward and opposite to the left foot. The right hand draws back to the rear side of the right flank at the same time with the left hand. The eyes look at the left forefinger. The body folds back like lying prostrate on the ground. This is a very low stance. After the body twists back, the lower abdomen is on the left thigh. When these motions seem almost complete, step forward again. This is called the starting action of drawing water in the swallow style.

Swallow - Drawing Water Form

Section Three

The Drawing Water Form of Swallow

The right hand goes forward to the underside of the left hand with its fist heart upward. Then the left hand turns to the underside of the right hand with its fist heart downward. Both wrists are in criss-cross. The changing begins at the time when the foregoing motions seem to be almost complete but actually not yet complete. This is called the middle action of the drawing water form of the swallow.

Swallow - Drawing Water Form

Section Four

The Drawing Water Form
of Swallow

The right fist heart twists outward. Both hands lift up to the shoulders at the same time. The eyes look to the center of the cross. The right foot steps forward at its utmost. When the right foot has not yet stepped down on the ground, the left foot lifts up and leans closely to the right shin. In the meantime, both hands separate from each other forward and backward from the top to draw a half circle and end opposite to each other at the shoulder level. This is like the stance of "white crane spreading wings." The eyes look to the front hand. This is called the end action of the drawing water form of the swallow. Students should know that the beginning, middle, and the end actions of the drawing water form of the swallow should be performed continuously.

Swallow - Form

Section Five

The Golden Cock Pecking Rice Form of Swallow

The right hand falls and beats forward in a straight manner. It is the same movement as in the golden cock pecking the rice. The steps of the feet are also the same.

Section Six

The Splitting Fist Form of Swallow

Then, the left hand and foot go forward, and the right hand draws backward. Perform the splitting fist and stop.

Section Seven

The Turning Back Form
of Swallow

The turning back motion is the same as that in the splitting fist. Make it stable. The following motion is "the golden cock shaking the feathers." The times of the performance depends on the case.

Section Eight

The Form
of Swallow

The closing should be done at the original starting place. It is the same with that of the splitting fist. Make the posture stable and then rest.

Chapter Nine

The Study of
Snake Form
(She Xing)

蛇
形

General Principle

The Study of Snake Form

The snake is the most maneuverable among animals. It has the ability to disperse grass. The decree of Heaven can be revealed by the fight between two snakes. The snake can bend and stretch, wind and roll. In human body, it is the *Yang* of the kidney. In the *Yi Jing*, it is the One of *Kan¹*. In the boxing, it is called the snake style. This style can activate the waist and has the meaning of "the rubbing between *Yin* and *Yang*" recorded in *Yi Jing²*. When the style is performed mildly, the internal real *Yang* seeps through the body outward. The spirit is so bright and penetrative that nothing can overspread it. If it is performed erroneously, the body is restricted by the *Qi* of *Yin* and confined by the clumsy force. Hence the bright spirit is blocked and perished. The wonderful effects of the snake style can be obtained only through exerting one's efforts with insistency in training.

Footnotes:

1) *Kan* is one of the eight diagrams in the Ba Gua and represents water. (T)

2) The form comes from the formless, this is a natural phenomenon of nature. *Yin* and *Yang* combine to produce form, its changes produce all creation. The sixty-four hexagrams are arranged around a central focus. One must practice with a balance of *Yin* and *Yang* in order to succeed.

Section One

The Beginning Form of Snake

The starting is from the trinity. First, the left foot makes a pad-step forward. Then the right hand penetrates to the underside of the left flank along the body with its hand heart upward. The right shoulder seems to go in the left armpit. Then the left hand bends back to the right shoulder. The left hand heart seems to hook on the tip of the right shoulder. The body goes down with the coincidence between *Yin* and *Yang*. The lower abdomen sits on the root of the left thigh.

Snake - Beginning Form

Section Two

The Advancing Form
of Snake

The right foot goes to the left shin without falling down to the ground and continuously goes slantingly to the right forward. When the right foot goes slantingly to the right forward, the right hand goes out too with its hand heart inward. Then make a following step as that in the tiger style. At the same time, the left hand draws back to the rear side of the left flank with its hand heart downward. Both hands are opposite each other forward and backward. Both shoulders and both hips open strength outward. The eyes look forward through the tip of the forefinger of the front hand.

Snake - Advancing Form

Section Three

The Changing Form of Snake

Perform the left form again. The motions of the left form are the same as the right form but on the left side. The repetitions of the performance depend on the space.

Snake - Changing Form

Section Four

The Turning Back Form of Snake

The turning back should be done after the right form. The right hand bends back to the left shoulder. The motions of the limbs and the body are the same as in the turning over of the sparrow hawk. The only difference between them is that the turning over of the sparrow hawk goes in the proper direction, i.e. south and north, or east and west; while the turning back of the snake goes in the oblique angle. The further advance is the same with the left form.

Snake - Turning Back Form

Section Five

The Closing Form
of Snake

The closing is the same with the turning back.   Hold it stable before resting.

Chapter Ten

The Study of Tai Bird Form (Tai Xing)

鮐形

General Principle

The Study of Tai Bird

The tai bird has a straight forward disposition and the ability to set up its tail. It can fly high when going up and both wings can hit an object with the speed and force like an arrow when falling down. In the body, this style can smooth the liver and strengthen the *Qi*. Hence it is helpful for the liver and lungs. In the boxing, it is called the tai bird style. It can activate both shoulders and feet. When it is performed mildly, it promotes the smoothed liver and the strengthened internal *Qi* that makes the chest empty and the belly solid. The empty chest and the solid belly are the path leading to the real principle of unification. If the style is performed erroneously, both shoulders are restrained and the chest stuffed up. Thus the internal *Qi* is blocked. That is to say that the path leading to the real principle of unification is blocked.

Section One

The Beginning Form
of Tai Bird

The starting is from the trinity. The left tiptoe twists outward. The body faces the proper direction. The left hand bends back. Both hands turn into fists with the fist heart inward opposite the navel. The arms lean against the abdomen.

Tai Bird - Beginning Form

Section Two

The Advancing Form
of Tai Bird

Both hands separate from each other to the left and right side and fall down like the white crane spreading wings. Both elbows lean on the flanks. Both fists rest on the underside of the flanks of each side. Both shoulders draw strength downward. When both hands separate from each other, the right foot steps slantingly forward. The left foot goes to the right foot and lifts up in contact with the right shin. The waist draws strength down. Hold the stance for a short while.

Tai Bird - Advancing Form

Section Three

The Advancing Form
of Tai Bird

    Both hands stretch straight forward from the flank of each side with the fist heart upward. The distance between both fists is about two or three inches. In the meantime, the left foot steps forward. Both shoulders draw strength downward and backward on the sly. The eyes look to the center of both fists. The right foot makes a following step as that in the tiger style. Make the posture stable before changing.

Tai Bird - Advancing Form

Section Four

The Changing Form of Tai Bird

The left foot makes a pad-step with its tiptoe hooking in a little bit. Both fists, as mentioned in the former form, are at the navel opposite with each other; then separate from each other in the manner of "the white crane spreading wings." Both fists fall down and lean on the underside of the flanks on each side. Both shoulders draw strength down. The right foot goes to the left shin and leans tightly to it. The waist should draw strength down. Hold the stance for a short while and then advance again.

Tai Bird - Changing Form

Section Five

The Advancing Form of Tai Bird

Both fists go straight out with the left foot. The eyes look to the center between both fists and the rest is as described in section three.

Tai Bird - Advancing Form

Section Six

The Closing Form
of Tai Bird

The closing is the same as the changing form. Make the posture stable before resting.

Chapter Eleven

The Study of Eagle Form (Ying Xing)

鷹形

General Principle

The Study of Eagle Form

The eagle has the most fierce and violent characteristics with the special abilities of capture and acute vision. It has its *Yang* outside and *Yin* inside. In human body, this style can raise the *Qi* of *Yang* from the kidney to the brain. The *Dan Shu* said that the internal real *Qi* arises from the *Ni Wan*, penetrates the three barriers and goes through the vertebrae. In the boxing, it is called the eagle style. When it is performed mildly, the real essence comes up and supplements the brain and makes the eyes have acute vision. If it is performed erroneously, the real strength cannot go through the limbs and the fire of *Yin* lifts up. This will result in dizziness of the head and a pair of redish eyes. The benefits of restoring the internal *Qi* of the pure *Yang* can be achieved through practicing this style correctly and diligently.

Footnotes:

1) The three barriers, or gates, are along the Ren/Du meridians. These points are places the Qi has trouble passing. The first is the *Yu Jen* point behind the head. The second is the *Lu Lu* point in the center of the back and the third is the place the fire and water meet at the coccyx.

Section One

The Beginning Form
of Eagle

The starting is from the trinity. All motions of the limbs and the body are the same as those in the splitting fist. The only difference between them is that in the eagle style, both hands imitate the claws of the eagle to catch its object; while in the splitting fist, both hands imitate the ax to split something. That is why it is called the eagle style here.

Eagle - Beginning Form

Chapter Twelve

The Study of Bear Form (Xiong Xing)

熊形

General Principle

The Study of Bear Form

The bear has the most obtuse property and the most majestic appearance with the special force to set upright its neck. It has its *Yin* outside and *Yang* inside. In the human body, this style can draw the *Qi* of *Yin* down back to the *Dan Tian*. In the boxing, it is called the bear style. This style can strengthen the neck and restore the *Qi* of pure *Yin*. The *Qi* of the bear style can be connected with the *Qi* of the eagle style and become *Yang* when ascending and *Yin* when descending. To perform these two styles together, it is called the battle of fighting will between the eagle and bear, and also called the friction between *Yin* and *Yang*. Actually the ascending and descending of *Yin* and *Yang* are but the stretching and contracting of *Qi*. To practice the dragon and tiger style respectively is called "opening." Here, to practice the eagle and bear style in connection is called "enclosing." To learn and understand the principle of opening and enclosing of the twelve styles is the path leading to the unification.

Bear - Beginning Form

Section One

The Beginning Form of Bear

The starting is from the trinity (see opposite page). The left hand falls down as in the splitting fist, then draws back to the lower abdomen and drills up along the belly to the level of the eyebrow. Meanwhile, the left foot draws back to the right foot. The left heel is opposite the right shin with its tiptoe on the ground and the heel up. The waist draws strength down. The eyes look up to the hand heart. The neck is upright. Both shoulders draw strength down. This is why it is said that the bear has erecting force of the neck.

Next, the right hand lifts up along the body to the left hand and then goes forward and downward like the eagle's claw catching something. The right arm seems bent but has strength. At the same time, the left hand draws back to the left flank as in the splitting fist (see opposite page). The left foot goes out with the right hand. The right hand goes between both legs. The right hand is aligned with the left foot. The right tiptoe contacts with the ground with its heel lifted. The eyes look to the root of the right thumb and the middle fingertip. Both hips enclose the crotch. The body seems relaxed but is also tightening, seems open but is also enclosing. Keep it stable before changing.

Bear - Beginning Form

Section Two

The Right Form
of Bear

The right hand falls down and drills up like the left hand in the left form (see photo on the previous page). When the right hand drills up, the left foot makes a pad-step. Then the left hand and right foot go out as described in the left form (see photos below). The repetitions of the performance depend on the space.

Bear - The Right Form

Section Three

The Turning Back Form of Bear

The right tiptoe hooks inward at its utmost. The left hand bores down and lifts up with the left foot. The body turns left. Then the right hand and the left foot go out. The rest is the same with what is described in the left and right form of the bear style.

Section Four

The Closing Form
of Bear

The closing should be at the original place. All motions are the same as in the turning back style.   Hold the posture stable before resting.

Chapter Thirteen

The Study of
the Twelve Forms
United into One

十 二 形 全 體 合 一 學

(Za Shi Chui - Mixed Form Beating)

雜 式 捶

General Principle

The Study of the Twelve Forms United Into One

Za Shi Chui is also called "integral fist." It is the integration of the whole five key links (five elements) and the twelve items (twelve animals). Practicing this form can make the body an integral unit without any deficit. The book *Da Xue*[1] indicates that we have to understand and master the whole so as to reach perfection. In the boxing, the inner and outer strength of four limbs and every bone is pure and in coincidence with each other. When the boxing is performed mildly, the internal *Qi* can flow to and fro in endless circulation and fill up the whole body without any gap. The book *Zhong Yong* indicates that marvellous change results from reaching the highest integrity. While reaching this level, the unseen strength flows and fills up everywhere in the body with coincidence between both the internal and the external[2]. The so-called internal strength forms inside the body and generates outward power naturally. The old masters said that arriving at this level is entering into a realm of performing the boxing without boxing, mastering boxing without intention, and the real idea exists in no mood[3].

Footnotes:

1) *Da Xue* is one of the classical works of the Ru school. It was written in the time between Ching and Han Dynasty, i.e. about 200 years B.C. (T)

2) The interplay of *Yin* and *Yang*, expansion and contraction, change without end. In boxing, this refers to the pure *Jing* which on cannot see or hear, but it exists. It flows smoothly inside and out. The *Qi* is always full throughout the body.

3) When one reaches the stage of the upper and lower connected and the internal and external united, you may use the art as your wish. The body will naturally adhere the rules, this is the true intent. Even though it is unseen, the result has already been achieved. You do not see it move, but it has changed already. All you do is follow the way.

Section One

The Shrinking Form of
Za Shi Chui

The starting point is trinity. After starting, perform the shrinking of the sparrow hawk style (Part II, Chapter 7, Section 1). Then stop.

Za Shi Chui - Shrinking Form

Section Two

The Flying into the Forest Form of Za Shi Chui

Stepping forward again, perform the "flying into the forest" form of the sparrow hawk style (Part II, Chapter 7, Section 2). The left fist stretches out in the front and the right fist is at the center of the forehead. Make it stable.

Za Shi Chui - Flying into the Forest

Section Three

Splitting Fist with Step Back Form of Za Shi Chui

The right hand falls down to the side of the navel from the forehead with its elbow in contact with the flank. In the meantime, the left hand draws back to the left flank and the left foot steps back to the rear side of the right leg. The legs are in the splitting fist stance. This form is called the "splitting fist with stepping back."

**Za Shi Chui - Splitting Fist
with Step Back**

Section Four

Splitting Fist with Step Back Form of Za Shi Chui

The left hand drills to the left side of the forehead. Then wipes down to the left flank in an open palm and stops at the left side of the navel. In the meantime, the right foot steps back to the rear side of the left foot. This stance is still like the splitting fist with stepping back in left form. Practice the left and the right form a total of four times. Then stop.

**Za Shi Chui - Splitting Fist
with Step Back**

Section Five

The Black Dragon Sucking Water Upside Down Form of Za Shi Chui

The right hand moves down and backward from the flank and turns up and forward to the forehead . It then falls down along the body to the navel. This is just like drawing a circle. In the meantime, the left hand drills up from the left flank through the outside of the right hand, with its heart inward, to the forehead. The distance between the hand and the forehead is about two or three inches. Next, the right arm moves up with its hand heart outward and stops with its hand back in contact with the forehead. Then the left hand falls down along the body to the navel with the hand heart facing upward. The body faces to the proper direction. Then stop. This style is called "the black dragon sucking water upside down."

Za Shi Chui - Black Dragon Sucking Water Upside Down

Section Six

The Spreading Single Wing Form of Za Shi Chui

The left foot steps back to the rear side of the right foot. Then the right foot steps back to the left foot. The right heel is properly opposite the left shin. In the meantime, the right hand falls down to the lower abdomen. The elbow and the fist are in close contact with the abdomen. The left fist stays at the left flank without moving. The waist draws strength down. The right part of the lower abdomen sits down on the thigh. The body shouldn't bend too much. The nose should be in line with the tiptoe as in looking downward. *Yin* and *Yang* are in coincidence with each other in the body. The shoulders and the hips draw strength as before. The eyes follow the right hand. When the movement stops, the eyes look forward. This style is called "the phoenix spreading single wing."

**Za Shi Chui - Spreading
Wing Form**

Section Seven

The Hiding Dragon Coming Out Form of Za Shi Chui

Advancing again, the right foot steps forward. In the meantime, the left hand stretches out. The left foot makes a following-step like that in the smashing fist. The stance is also like that of the smashing fist. Advance again after stopping. This style is called "the hiding dragon coming out."

**Za Shi Chui - The Hiding
Dragon Coming Out Form**

Section Eight

The Black Tiger Going Out of the Cave Form of Za Shi Chui

All motions are the same as those of "the black tiger going out of the cave" form in the linking of the five fists (Part I, Chapter 6, Section 3). Make it stable and then advance.

**Za Shi Chui - Black Tiger
Going Out of the Cave Form**

Section Nine

The White Crane Spreading Wings Form of Za Shi Chui

All motions are the same as in the "white crane spreading wings form" in the linking of the five fists (Part I, Chapter 6, Section 4). Make it stable and then advance.

**Za Shi Chui - White Crane
Spreading Wings**

Section Ten

The Pounding Fist Form of Za Shi Chui

All motions are the same as in the pounding fist. Make it stable and then advance.

Za Shi Chui - Pounding Fist Form

Section Eleven

The Spreading Double Wings Form of Za Shi Chui

Both hands fall down to the lower abdomen. The right fist rolls in with its fist heart upward and falls down into the left palm. Both elbows closely contact with their flanks. The body as if it is bound. In the meantime, the right foot makes a back pad-step with its tiptoe slanting outward. The eyes look forward. This style is called "the phoenix spreading double wings." Stop and then advance.

Za Shi Chui - Spreading Double Wings Form

251

Section Twelve

The Flying into the Forest Form of Za Shi Chui

All motions are the same as in the style of "the sparrow hawk flying into the forest" (Part II, Chapter 7, Section Two). Make it stable and then advance.

Za Shi Chui - Flying into the Forest Form

Za Shi Chui - Splitting Fist with Step Back

Section Thirteen

The Splitting Fist with Step Back and the Black Dragon Sucking Water Forms of Za Shi Chui

This is also known as the "splitting fist upside down with a back step." The movement is as before (sections 3 and 4). When stepping back to the end, change into the style of the "black dragon sucking water upside down." Advance after only a short stop.

Za Shi Chui - Splitting Fist with Step Back

Za Shi Chui - Black Dragon Sucking Water

Section Fourteen

The Swallow Drawing Water Form of Za Shi Chui

At the end of the black dragon sucking water, when the right hand comes forward and falls down, closely follow with the form of the "drawing water form" of the swallow. Then stop. Refer to the figure of the swallow style (Part II, Chapter 8, Sections 2 - 4).

Za Shi Chui - Swallow Drawing Water Form

Za Shi Chui - Swallow Drawing Water Form

Section Fifteen

The Smashing Fist Form of Za Shi Chui

Advancing again, perform the smashing fist. The motions of the hands and feet are the same with the first stance in the first style of the linking fists (Part I, Chapter 6, Section 1).

Za Shi Chui - Swallow Drawing Water Form

Za Shi Chui - Smashing Fist Form

Section Sixteen

The Blue Dragon Going Out of the Water Form of Za Shi Chui

Stepping back and stretching out the hands again, the motions are the same as in the style of "the blue dragon coming out of water" in the linking fists (Part I, Chapter 6, Section 2).

**Za Shi Chui - Blue Dragon
Coming Out of the Water Form**

Section Seventeen

The Black Tiger Coming Out of its Cave Form of Za Shi Chui

Advancing again, perform the style of "the black tiger coming out of its cave" in the linking fists (Part 1, Chapter 6, Section 3). Make it stable and then change.

**Za Shi Chui - Black Tiger
Coming Out of its Cave**

Section Eighteen

The White Crane Spreading Wings Form of Za Shi Chui

Changing form, perform the style of the "white crane spreading wings" of the linking fists (Part 1, Chapter 6, Section 4). Make it stable and advance again.

**Za Shi Chui - White Crane
Spreading Wings Form**

Section Nineteen

The Pounding Fist Form of Za Shi Chui

Advancing again, perform the pounding fist. Make it stable and advance again.

**Za Shi Chui -
Pounding Fist Form**

Section Twenty

The Spreading Double Wings Form of Za Shi Chui

Changing again, perform the style of "the phoenix spreading double wings" (see Section 11). Make it stable.

**Za Shi Chui - Spreading
Double Wings Form**

Section Twenty-One

The Flying into the Forest Form of Za Shi Chui

All motions are the same as in the style of "the sparrow hawk flying into the forest" (Part II, Chapter 7, Section 2). Make it stable and then advance.

Za Shi Chui - Flying into the Forest Form

Section Twenty-Two

The Splitting Fist with Step Back and the Black Dragon Sucking Water Forms of Za Shi Chui

This is also known as the "splitting fist upside down with a back step." The movement is as before (sections 3 and 4). When stepping back to the end, change into the style of the "black dragon sucking water upside down." Advance after only a short stop.

Za Shi Chui - Splitting Fist with Step Back

Za Shi Chui - Splitting Fist with Step Back

Section Twenty-Three

The Blue Dragon Stretching Out its Claws Form of Za Shi Chui

The right hand stretches forward at the level of the eyes from the forehead with the fingers separated. Both feet stand still. Both shoulders relax and draw strength. After only a short stop, repeat the left hand again. This style is called "the blue dragon stretching out the claws."

Za Shi Chui - Black Dragon Sucking Water

Za Shi Chui - Blue Dragon Stretching Out its Claws

Section Twenty-Four

The Eagle Claw Form of Za Shi Chui

The left hand stretches out toward the upper side of the right hand from the heart. The right hand draws back to the right flank. Both feet stand still. The motions of both hands are just like the eagle catching something with its claws. This style is called "the eagle claw form."

**Za Shi Chui -
Eagle Claw Form**

Section Twenty-Five

The Wrapping Hands Form of Za Shi Chui

The left hand wraps back just like the wrapping up of the linking fists form (Part I, Chapter 6, Section 7). The right hand keeps at the right flank without moving. Then make a slight stop. This style is called "the wrapping hands."

Note: The photo below shows the opposite side. In this form the left hand wraps forward and the right hand back as in the explanation above. Otherwise the posture is the same.

**Za Shi Chui -
Wrapping Hands Form**
(Note: Photo is showing opposite side - in this form the left hand wraps forward and the right hand is back as explained above

Section Twenty-Six

The Pushing the Window to See the Moon Form of Za Shi Chui

Changing forms, the left wrist twists strength outward and stretches slantingly outward and upward. In the meantime, the left foot steps out. The body draws strength down into a low stance. Both legs are in the horse back riding posture. The left shoulder wraps inward, relaxes, and draws strength. The eyes look between the thumb and the forefinger of the left hand. The right hand stays at the right flank without moving. Then stop. This form is called "pushing the window to see the moon."

**Za Shi Chui - Pushing the
Window to See the Moon**

Section Twenty-Seven

The Three Basins Sink to the Ground Form of Za Shi Chui

Changing form, the left hand bends back and falls down to the level of the root of the thigh. The distance between the left hand and the thigh is about two or three inches. The wrist twists strength outward. The elbow forms a half circle. The right hand falls down and the right wrist twists strength outward at the same time. Both legs are still in the horse riding form without moving. The eyes look to the left-forward direction. Both shoulders relax and draw strength outward. The waist draws strength downward. This style is called "the three basins sink to the ground."

**Za Shi Chui - Three Basins
Sink to the Ground Form**

Section Twenty-Eight

The Lazy Dragon Lying on the Road Form of Za Shi Chui

Advancing again, the left hand stretches forward with strength at its utmost to the level of the heart. Then the hand rolls into a fist and the wrist twists strength inward with the fist heart upward. Then the hand wraps back with wrapping strength to the heart with its elbow contacting the flank tightly.

When the left hand wraps back, the right hand stretches out over the left hand with its fist heart upward. At this time, the left fist heart turns downward. The right foot steps out at the same time as the right hand. The stepping and the leg postures are the same as in the dragon style (Part II, Chapter 1, Section 2). The eyes look forward along the right hand. Both shoulders draw strength downward and outward. Take a slight rest. This is called "the lazy dragon lying on the road."

Za Shi Chui - Lazy Dragon Lying on the Road Form

Section Twenty-Nine

The Black Dragon Overturning the River Form of Za Shi Chui

Advancing again, the left leg steps forward as in "the sparrow hawk flying into the forest" form. In the meantime, the left hand strikes out from the under side of the right hand and the right hand draws back at the same time. Both hands are the same posture as in the crossing fist. The eyes look to the front hand. Then stop. This is called "the black dragon overturning the river."

**Za Shi Chui - Black Dragon
Overturning the River Form**

Section Thirty

The Smashing Fist Form of Za Shi Chui

Advancing again, the right hand stretches out. The posture is the same as that of the smashing fist. Both feet stay in place. Then stop.

**Za Shi Chui -
Smashing Fist Form**

Section Thirty-One

The Dragon and the Tiger Meeting Each Other Form of Za Shi Chui

The right foot lifts up and forward to the level of the heart as if to draw a half circle. The left hand stretches forward in parallel with the right foot at the same time. This is called "the dragon and the tiger meeting each other." Then stop.

**Za Shi Chui - Dragon and Tiger
Meeting Each Other Form**

271

Section Thirty-Two

The Black Tiger Coming Out of its Cave Form of Za Shi Chui

Advancing again, the right foot falls down to the front. The right hand stretches out and the left hand draws back. It is performed the same as "the black tiger coming out of the cave" form (Part 1, Chapter 6, Section 3). Make a stop.

**Za Shi Chui - Black Tiger
Coming Out of its Cave Form**

Section Thirty-Three

The White Crane Spreading Wings Form of Za Shi Chui

Changing form, perform the style of the "white crane spreading wings" of the linking fists (Part 1, Chapter 6, Section 4). Make it stable and advance again.

Za Shi Chui - White Crane Spreading Wings Form

Section Thirty-Four

The Pounding Fist Form
of Za Shi Chui

Changing again, perform the pounding fist. Make a slight stop.

**Za Shi Chui -
Pounding Fist Form**

Section Thirty-Five

The Spreading Double Wings Form of Za Shi Chui

Changing again, perform the style of "the phoenix spreading double wings" (see Section 11).   Make it stable.

**Za Shi Chui - Spreading
Double Wings Form**

Section Thirty-Six

The Flying into the Forest Form of Za Shi Chui

Advancing again, perform the "sparrow hawk flying into the forest" form. Make a stop. This is also called "the pounding fist with follow through steps."

| Za Shi Chui - Flying into the Forest Form | Za Shi Chui - Splitting Fist with Step Back |

Section Thirty-Seven

The Splitting Fist with Step Back and the Black Dragon Sucking Water Forms of Za Shi Chui

Retreating again, perform the "reversed splitting fist." Once the form returns to the original place, begin the style of "the black dragon sucking water upside down." Make a stop.

Za Shi Chui - Splitting Fist with Step Back

Za Shi Chui - Black Dragon Sucking Water

Section Thirty-Eight

The Spreading Single Wing Form of Za Shi Chui

Retreating again, perform "the phoenix spreading single wing" form. Make a stop.

**Za Shi Chui - Spreading
Single Wing Form**

Section Thirty-Nine

The Hiding Dragon Coming Out Form of Za Shi Chui

Advancing again, it is the style of "the hiding dragon coming out" (See Section 7).

**Za Shi Chui - Hiding
Dragon Coming Out Form**

Section Forty

The Black Tiger Coming Out of its Cave Form of Za Shi Chui

Advancing again, perform "the black tiger coming out of the cave" form (Part 1, Chapter 6, Section 3). Make a stop.

**Za Shi Chui - Black Tiger
Coming Out of its Cave**

Section Forty-One

The Lotus Leaves Swaying in the Wind Form of Za Shi Chui

Both hands fall down from the front and move along the left side from the bottom to the top as in drawing a circle. After coming back from the rear side, both hands move through the front at eye level and push to the right front with both palms standing at the level of the eyebrow. The right hand stretches out straight at its utmost and the left hand is at the right shoulder. The right foot steps back following both hands. Both legs form a scissors type stance. Both hands push back. The eyes look back along with both hands. Both shoulders draw strength like before. Make a slight stop. This is called "the lotus leaves swaying in the wind."

Za Shi Chui - Lotus Leaves Swaying in the Wind Form

Section Forty-Two

The Pointing Out the Road Form of Za Shi Chui

Advancing again, the right hand swings around to the front of the body and pulls back to the right flank. At the same time, the left fist stretches down and forward from the right shoulder coming over the right fist as in the smashing fist. The left foot and the left hand stretch out at the same time. This step is the same as in the smashing fist but without the following-step of the rear foot.

**Za Shi Chui - Pointing Out
the Road Form**

Section Forty-Three

The Black Tiger Coming Out of its Cave Form of Za Shi Chui

Advancing again, perform "the black tiger coming out of the cave" form (Part 1, Chapter 6, Section 3). Then turn back at once without any stop.

.

**Za Shi Chui - Black Tiger
Coming Out of its Cave**

Section Forty-Four

The Closing After Turning Back Form of Za Shi Chui

The turning back is performed in the style of the "sparrow hawk turning over" (Part II, Chapter 7, Section 4). Make a stop and stand at attention. Then rest.

**Za Shi Chui -
Turning Back Form**

Chapter Fourteen

The Study of
the Whole
in Application

十二形全體大用學

(An Shen Pao Quan - Stable Body Pounding)

安身炮拳

General Principle

The Study of the Whole in Application

An Shen Pao means that everything developed from and raised by the heaven and earth is in its own proper place. In the human body, the internal *Qi*, is always filling up the whole body whether it is large or small. As for its application out of the body, the internal *Qi* can have its function without manifesting itself, cause change without moving itself, and make results without its own action. Anyone who has this internal *Qi* at a high level can feel the great virtue and perform according to the real principles. In the boxing, these are the large and small virtues. The large virtue is the strength which is manifest when outside and inside coincide. It is a kind of endless power. The small virtue is the change in the boxing. It is also endless just like water gushing out from a fountain. In this way, the real principle of Xing Yi boxing is to perform the boxing without boxing, to master the boxing without intention, and that the real idea exists in "no mood." Reaching to this level, it is realizable that the internal strength in the Xing Yi boxing is the principle of heaven and earth, the property of human beings, and the *Jing Dan* in Taoism. There are different names such as strength, principle, property, and the *Jing Dan*, but they have the same principle. The strength in the boxing can coincide with the principle of different related categories and can reach to the same high level. It can coincide with the virtue of heaven and earth, with the brightness of the sun and the moon, with the sequence of four seasons, and with the luck of the spirits. This is the goal of the endeavor of all students.

Section One

An Shen Pao Quan

Two persons *A* and *B* practice together. *A* is the first one and *B* is the second one. *A*'s starting point is trinity. *B*'s starting point is also trinity. *A*'s left hand slaps-off *B*'s left hand and makes a smashing fist with the right hand instantly. *B* draws back his right foot , lifts up the left foot in contact with the right leg, pushes away *A*'s right hand with his left hand and makes a smashing fist with a swift step forward .

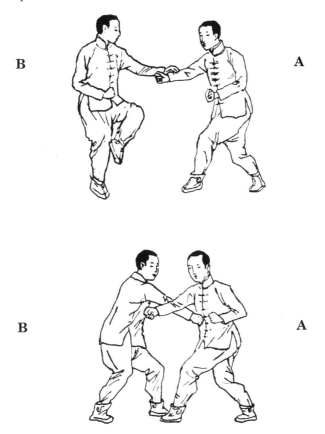

Section Two

An Shen Pao Quan

A pulls *B*'s right hand with his own right hand and splits *B*'s face with both left and right hands without moving his feet. *B* draws back and raises his right hand and hits *A*'s heart with both left and right hands in the style of "the sparrow hawk flying into the forest." *A* makes a cross pad-step with the left foot. The right foot steps to the outside of *B*'s left foot. The left hand bends back and pulls *B*'s left hand. The right hand splits *B*'s face at the same time in the style of splitting fist.

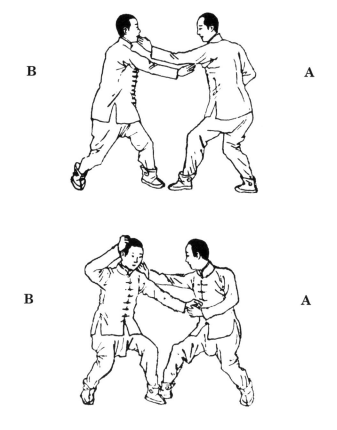

B   A

B   A

Section Three

An Shen Pao Quan

B makes a cross pad-step with the left foot. The right foot steps forward instantly. The left hand draws back and lifts up. In the meantime, the right hand splits *A*'s face on the left side. *A* wraps strength inward with the right hand with the hand heart upward. The left wrist twists strength outward with the hand heart downward with a distance of one or two inches from the face. Both hands go forward to cut *B*'s right arm. This is called "the double cut hands." In the meantime, the right foot steps forward.

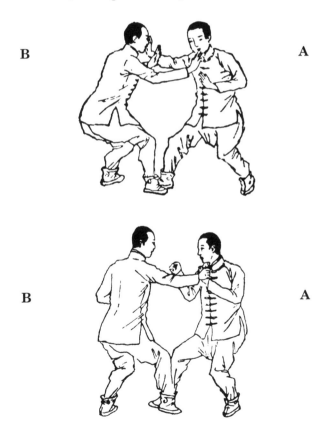

Section Four

An Shen Pao Quan

B splits *A*'s face with the left hand and draws back the right hand to the heart. *A* changes into the right "double cut hands." It is the same as the left one described previously. Then *A*'s right hand stretches out underneath his own left hand and hits *B*'s heart without moving the feet.

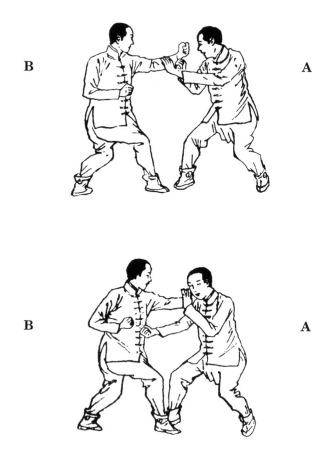

Section Five

An Shen Pao Quan

B draws back the left foot. The right foot lifts up. The right hand supports *A*'s right hand to lead him into emptiness. Then the left hand stretches out from underneath *A*'s wrist, pulls and pokes it backward. The right hand hits *A*'s heart immediately. Following the right hand, the right foot falls down to the ground. The actions of pulling, poking, and hitting of both hands should be done continuously without any break. *A* squats the waist down. The right hand brings *B*'s right hand backward from the top. The left hand goes to the front of the right hand and does as the right one. Then the right hand goes forward to grasp *B*'s face. The actions of bringing and grasping of both hands should be done continuously without any break.

Section Six

An Shen Pao Quan

B bends back his right hand swiftly and then drills with the right hand to *A*'s right hand. The left hand pulls back to the heart in a low body stance. *A* quickly parries *B*'s right arm up with the left arm. The right hand draws back and stretches out again to hit *B*'s heart. The left foot and the right hand go forward at the same time in the style of the pounding fist.

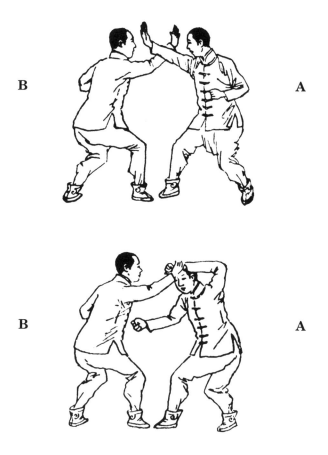

B   A

B   A

Section Seven

An Shen Pao Quan

B changes into splitting fist while stepping back. The left hand hooks *A*'s right hand. The right hand draws back to the heart with its hand heart downward. *A* parries *B*'s left hand off with his own left hand. The right hand strikes the left side *B*'s face with the back of the hand. The right foot and the right hand go forward at the same time.

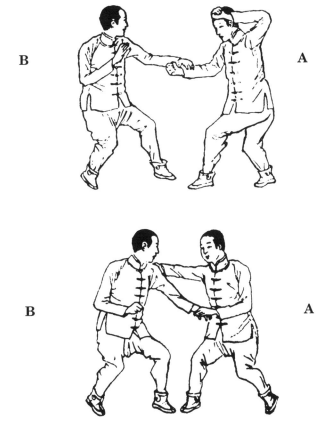

Section Eight

An Shen Pao Quan

B draws back his right foot. Following it, the left foot steps back too. This is called the "double stepping back." The left hand draws back and drills out again swiftly. The actions of the hands and the feet should be at the same time. *A* steps forward with the right foot immediately. The left foot makes a following-step. The left hand slaps away *B*'s left hand. The right hand splits the left side of *B*'s left from underneath *B*'s arm. This is called the "stealthily beating."

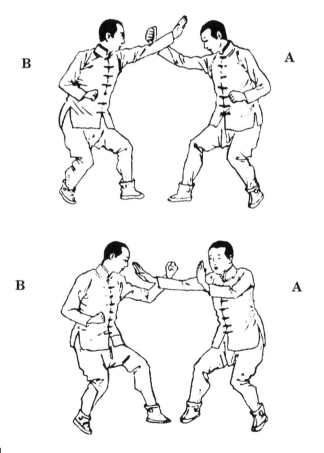

Section Nine

An Shen Pao Quan

B stretches forward with the right foot and steps down between A's legs. The right hand slaps away A's right hand. Then the left hand stretches forward to the front of the right hand and pokes A's right arm outward. At the time of the stepping down of the right foot, the right hand strikes the right side of A's face with a back hand strike. A bends back the right hand and drills out to the outside of B's right arm. The right foot steps back quickly. The right hand pulls B's right arm backward. At the time of the stepping back of the right foot, the left hand splits the right side of B's face.

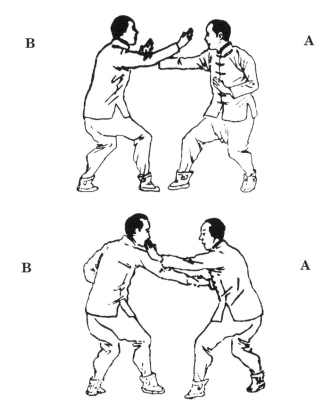

Section Ten

An Shen Pao Quan

B steps back with the left foot. The right hand removes *A*'s left hand. The right foot and the right hand lift up at the same time. The left hand pulls *A*'s arm downward. The right hand goes out to grab *A*'s head. *A* bends back the left arm and drills to the inside of *B*'s right hand. Then the right arm, in a shape of a snake, rushes forward to grab *B*'s crotch. The right foot and the right hand go forward at the same time.

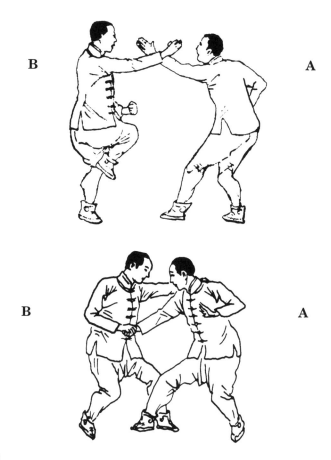

B   A

B   A

Section Eleven

An Shen Pao Quan

  B steps back with the right foot. The right hand pulls *A*'s right hand back and downward. The left hand stretches out swiftly to *A*'s neck and pulls it back with pressing strength at the same time with the pulling action of the right hand. *A* bends back the right hand and parries *B*'s left hand outward . The left hand splits again towards the right side of *B*'s face without moving the feet.

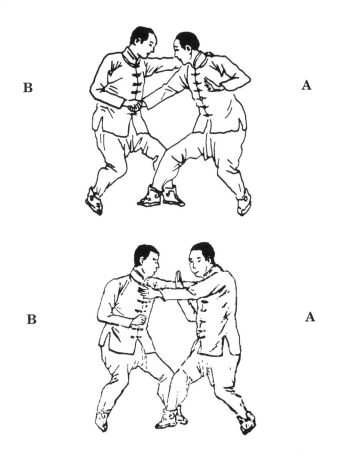

B   A

B   A

Section Twelve

An Shen Pao Quan

B draws back the left elbow to the flank. The right hand drills quickly toward the inside of *A*'s left hand without moving the feet. *A* draws back the left hand to the flank. The right hand splits toward the left side of *B*'s face without moving the feet.

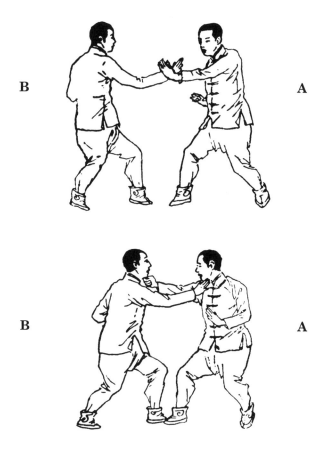

B   A

B   A

Section Thirteen

An Shen Pao Quan

B slaps *A*'s right hand with his right hand. The left hand strikes toward *A*'s right flank. The body changes into the horse riding stance. *A* squats down without moving the feet. Then both hands act as the "dragging rope" in the monkey style and grab *B*'s head with the right hand.

Section Fourteen

An Shen Pao Quan

B steps back with the left foot. The right hand changes into the drilling palm and drills toward the outside of *A*'s right hand. The left hand stops at the left flank. *A* pokes out *B*'s right hand from inside with the left hand and grips it with the elbow. The right hand cuts forward swiftly to the left side of *B*'s neck. In the meantime, the left leg goes forward and steps down at the outside of *B*'s right leg to tie him up.

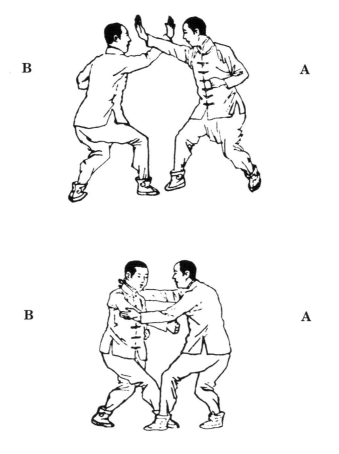

Section Fifteen

An Shen Pao Quan

B cuts off A's right hand with "double cutting hands" without moving the feet. A draws back the right hand. The left hand splits toward B's right face without moving the feet.

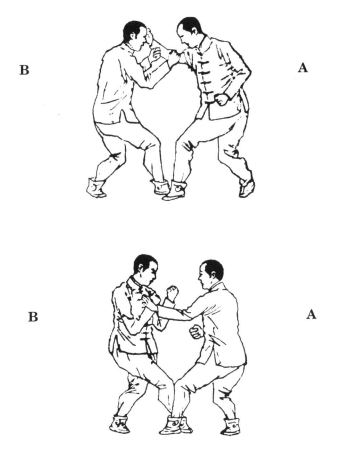

Section Sixteen

An Shen Pao Quan

B uses the "double cutting hands" again. Then the right hand strikes *A*'s left flank stealthily. *A* squats down without moving the feet. The left hand pulls *B*'s right arm following its force. This is called "to take away a sheep within one's reach."

B  A

B  A

Section Seventeen

An Shen Pao Quan

A maintains the squatting stance. The right foot kicks toward *B*'s right leg. The right hand grabs toward *B*'s right arm like the "dragging rope" in the monkey style, but the right foot lifts up before stepping down on the ground. The left foot and the right hand act at the same time like the style of "the leopard climbing the tree." *B* lifts up the right leg and moves it back, then puts it down. The right hand bends back and drills again toward the outside of *A*'s right hand. The left hand stops at the heart.

B   A

B   A

Section Eighteen

An Shen Pao Quan

A lifts up *B*'s right arm with his left hand. The right hand draws
back and splits toward the left side of *B*'s face without moving the
feet. *B* draws back the right hand quickly to the right flank. The left
hand grabs towards *A*'s right shoulder. This is called "the sparrow
hawk grabbing the shoulder."

B**A**

Section Nineteen

An Shen Pao Quan

A pulls *B*'s left wrist outward with the right hand. Closely following it the left hand pushes the top of *B*'s left wrist outward. Then the right hand splits toward the left side of *B*'s face without moving the feet. This is also the principle of "the dragging rope" in the monkey style. *B* bends back the left arm and drills toward the inside of *A*'s right hand and pokes it back. The right hand splits toward the left side of *A*'s face without moving the feet.

B   A

Section Twenty

An Shen Pao Quan

A cuts away *B*'s right hand with "double cutting hands" without moving the feet. *B* draws back the right hand and splits toward the left side of *A*'s face with the left hand without moving the feet.

B   A

Section Twenty-One

An Shen Pao Quan

A uses the "double cutting hands" again to cut away *B*'s left hand. The right hand makes a stealthy strike as before. This stealthy striking of the right hand is the same as the first action of the smashing fist performed by *B* at the opening.

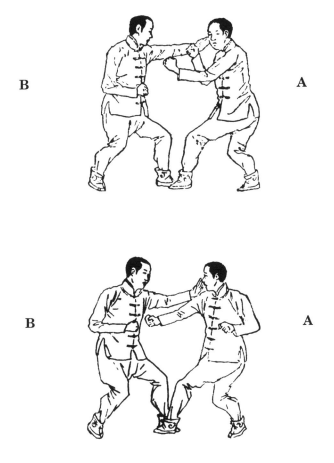

B   A

B   A

Section Twenty-Two

An Shen Pao Quan

B retreats the right foot and lifts up the left foot. The left hand pushes *A*'s right hand outward. The right hand strikes toward *A*'s belly with a smashing fist. This is the same as *A*'s first action in the opening. In the following performance, *B* will perform what *A* performed before and *A* will perform what *B* performed before. It can be performed continuously without end. When rest is necessary, go back to the original starting point and stop. Then rest.

B   A

Postscript

In the year of 1915, I fortunately had the chance to visit Mr. Sun Lu Tang and read his book *The Study of Xing Yi Boxing*. Under his instruction, I have understood the precious value of this set. It is mind inside and form outside. The *Qi* reaches where the mind goes. When self training and cultivating the internal *Qi* to a rather high level, one can reach the proper way of moderation. That which forms outside will naturally follow this principle. Both the metaphysical and physical sides meet each other in a coincidence. The way of persuing only outer things can never be comparable with this true contribution. These few words can only show my respect and admiration to Mr. Sun Lu Tang.

Wu Xing Gu at Dong Tai
April 1919

About the Translator

Mr. Albert Z. Liu received a fundamental training in Chinese traditional martial arts during his childhood. When he was a teenager, he studied Chinese traditional medicine and Tai Ji boxing. While studying biological medicine at the University of Nanking, at the age of about twenty, he learned the Ba Gua Tai Ji from Master Ma Quan, who was a student of Master Ma Yong Sheng and Master Ma Gui. While he studied philosophy at Peking University in the early 1950's, he practiced Tai Ji and Yue Jia boxing. The instructor was employed by the University.

After working as a translator in various foreign languages over a long period of time, he was received as a member of the Association of Medicine in Shanghai, and he was a member of the Shanghai Association of Scientific Technical Translators. He was also in charge of the translation group at the Research Institute of PC in Shanghai. While teaching at the Shanghai College, he was confirmed as an associate professor by the government and was engaged as a professor and nominated as the director of the first foreign languages section in the college. He has had numerous articles and publications published by the Shanghai Scientific Technical Documents Publishing House and the Shanghai Literature Translation Publishing House.

Mr. Liu's wife, Jane Yao, having learned internal martial arts from different masters, was a favorite student of Master Hao Shao Ru. After coming to the United States, Mr. Liu has been working part time together with Jane Yao in martial arts teaching and judging. During the translation of this book, he received help from Jane Yao on the distribution and shift of the internal strength in this set.

# NORTH AMERICAN TANG SHOU TAO

Individuals wishing to find out more about the art of Xing Yi Quan, or locate a Xing Yi instructor, should contact the North American Tang Shou Tao Association. North American Tang Shou Tao is the largest Xing Yi Quan association in North America with member schools and qualified instructors located throughout the United States.

In addition to its yearly full-contact Xing Yi Quan tournament and instructors conferences, North American Tang Shou Tao periodically sponsors teams to compete in full-contact tournaments in Taiwan, sponsors qualified instructors from Taiwan and Mainland China for seminar tours of the United States, and sponsors intensive group study trips in mainland China.

North American Tang Shou Tao is associated with the International Tang Shou Tao Association based in Taipei, Taiwan. Write to:

North American Tang Shou Tao
P. O. Box 36235
Tucson, AZ 85740